Tables

TABLES

Outstanding Projects from America's Best Craftsmen

WITH PLANS AND COMPLETE INSTRUCTIONS
FOR BUILDING 10 CLASSIC TABLES

ANTHONY GUIDICE

The Taunton Press

Publisher: Jim Childs
Associate publisher: Helen Albert
Associate editor: Strother Purdy
Editor: Paul Anthony
Copy editor: Candace B. Levy
Indexer: Susan G. Burke
Cover designer: Steve Hughes
Interior designer: Lori Wendin
Layout artist: Suzie Yannes
Photographer: Tom Cerniglio
Illustrator: Melanie Powell

The Taunton Press
Inspiration for hands-on living®

Printed in the United States of America
10 9 8 7 6 5 4

The Taunton Press, Inc.,
63 South Main Street, PO Box 5506, Newtown, CT 06470-5506
e-mail: tp@taunton.com

Library of Congress Cataloging-in-Publication Data
Guidice, Anthony.
    Tables : outstanding projects from America's best craftsmen : with plans and
complete instructions for building 10 classic tables / Anthony Guidice.
        p.   cm. — (Step-by-step)
    ISBN-13: 978-1-56158-342-3
    ISBN-10: 1-56158-342-1
    1. Tables. 2. Furniture making. I. Title.
TT197.5.T3 G85   2000
684.1'3—dc21   00-037395

ABOUT YOUR SAFETY

Working with wood is inherently dangerous. Using hand or power tools improperly or ignoring standard safety practices can lead to permanent injury or even death. Don't try to perform operations you learn about here (or elsewhere) unless you're certain they are safe for you. If something about an operation doesn't feel right, don't do it. Look for another way. We want you to enjoy the craft, so please keep safety foremost in your mind whenever you're working with wood.

ACKNOWLEDGMENTS

Woodworkers can always benefit from learning about the work of other craftsmen. Not only can we get design ideas but we can learn new techniques as well. I would like to thank the cabinetmakers whose work inspired some of the projects in this book: Arthur Chapin, John MacDonald, John Lavine, Frank Klausz, and Mario Rodriguez. Their designs have provided a nice mix of styles to this book and offer some interesting challenges to both new and experienced woodworkers.

Contents

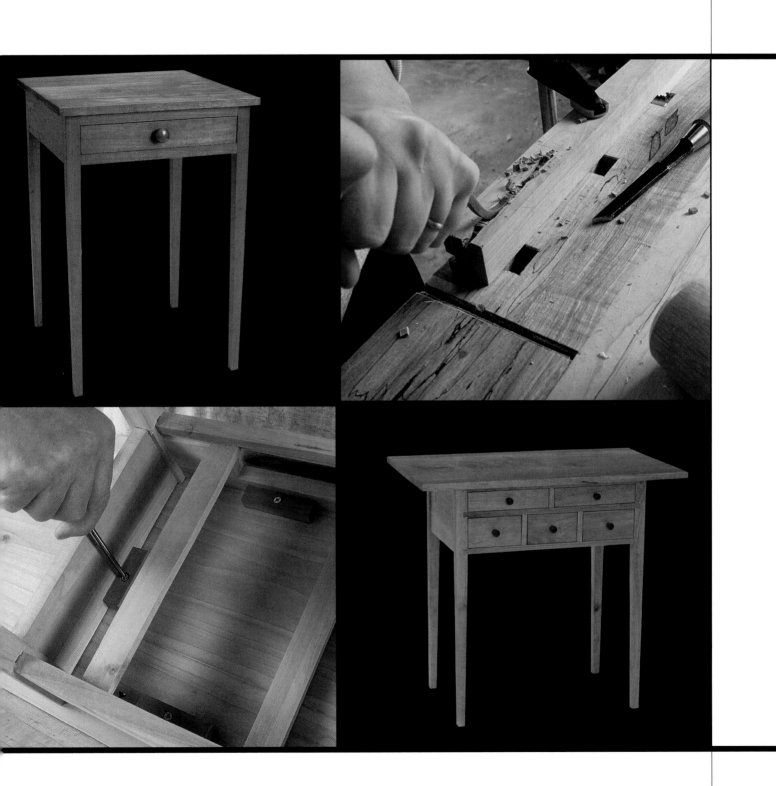

INTRODUCTION

The first time I really saw a table through a woodworker's eyes was when my teacher showed me a cherry end table he had built years before. He explained how the top must be high enough for the lamp to throw light, but not too high; that the legs have to be tapered or the proportions will look wrong; and how essential it is to fit the drawer to the guides accurately, or the drawer will bind and stick. He also described the advantages of an oil finish: it's soft and lustrous, the top won't stain if you set a glass on it, and the wood still looks like wood.

As always, I asked questions without trying to appear too stupid. Did you cut all this wood to size with a hand-saw? No, a table saw. Did you edge joint the top? No, I used a jointer plane for that—didn't have a jointer yet. What about the dovetails in the drawers? Hand cut, I think. There were only a few to do. Did you mortise and tenon the legs? He nodded. They've got to be strong to last.

In a simple well-made end table, there are myriad lessons in wood-working. This is why tables are great projects for any furniture maker, experienced or beginner. They can be challenging to make, but without the engineering gymnastics necessary in, say, building a chair. You can be flexible with the techniques you use to build them, without taking undue risks.

The table designs in this book were assembled from all over the United States and from all different types of woodworkers. There are a few traditional pieces, Shaker and Arts and Crafts, contemporary work from the Northeast and the West, and a few surprises included as well.

The range of projects offers a variety of approaches and techniques and the opportunity to learn a new skill, sharpen others, and possibly develop new ways of seeing. I hope you'll carry away something valuable, whether you've built hundreds of tables or are considering building your first.

Before you begin reading this book, I'd like to leave you with a few thoughts about workmanship. There seems to be a tendency among many contemporary woodworkers to fuss their furniture to death. Woodworking doesn't have to be flawlessly executed. Joints don't have to be cut perfectly. Just work as carefully as you can to get them fairly snug, and they should be fine. Of the dozens of tables I've made over many years, none of the joints was "perfect," but none has ever failed.

And don't worry about finessing the wood surfaces. How flat does a tabletop need to be? Flat enough so that a ball won't roll off it. As for tool marks, it's fine if some of them show. They just show the woodworker's hand in the piece.

TABLE-BUILDING BASICS

WHEN IT COMES TO making furniture, the world of tables offers the woodworker seemingly unlimited design possibilities. In its simplest form, a table may be nothing more than a plank resting on a packing crate. On the other hand, it can be as elaborate or as large as you care to make it, whether it's a carved beast of a banquet table or some tiny, inlaid pedestal designed to hold nothing heavier than a hairbrush.

Although a table can be made a thousand ways, it is a functional piece by nature. As such, you need to consider what it is to be used for, how best it will suit that purpose, and how big to make it. After that, you'll need to decide what materials to use and how to build it using the tools that you have. In this chapter, I'll discuss these issues, which should help you build a table of your own design or any of the tables in this book.

DESIGN CONSIDERATIONS

Tables are designed to support or hold items, whether dinnerware, lamps, art objects, or old newspapers. In fact, many tables have a specific function that dictates certain design parameters. For example, a dining table should be a comfortable height for eating, and a sewing table must be at the correct height for working. A hallway table should be narrow enough to allow walkway passage. And a table for children should have large, rounded corners to prevent injury.

Typical table forms

Although tables come in many designs, there are a few basic forms, with many variations. Three of the most common forms are represented in this book: four-legged tables with aprons, trestle tables, and pedestal tables.

Four-legged tables with aprons are probably the most common. The aprons are more than just a design element; they are an integral part of the structure, providing a means of stabilizing the legs and creating a support framework for the top. Frank Klausz's Sturdy Kitchen Table (p. 138) is an excellent example of this form. John Lavine's eight-legged Arts and Crafts Style Coffee Table (p. 110) is an unusual variation on the form.

A trestle table, at its simplest, is a top that spans two panels or sets of divergent legs that serve as supports. A stretcher beam typically connects the supports. Trestle construction is particularly popular for dining tables, because the lack of aprons allows more knee room. Mario Rodriguez's Danish Farmer's Trestle Table (p. 152) is a good example of this form.

Pedestal tables take an entirely different approach to the base. The top is supported by one or more central columns of some form, often terminating in feet at the bottom. The Shaker Candle Stand (p. 18) is a very basic pedestal table.

Table types and sizes

Although there are countless types of tables to suit specialized needs, there are some types that are commonly found in the typical household. I've listed a few here that are

Typical Apron Tables

Typical Trestle Tables

included in this book. Remember that any of these can be customized to suit your particular needs.

Kitchen and dining tables Typically, kitchen and dining tables are 29 in. or 30 in. high. When determining the tabletop length, allow about 30 in. side to side for each person. The width of the top should allow a minimum of 12 in. in front of each sitter and another 12 in. or so for serving dishes, making a 34-in.- to 36-in.-wide top a comfortable size for face-to-face dining.

A kitchen table is usually fairly small, often seating only four people, so you don't need a top of more than about 36 in. by 60 in. If you have a large family at home, a big trestle dining table might be a good solution. Just remember to include an overhang of about 18 in. at each end, so diners sitting those places don't bang their knees on the trestles. If you infrequently serve a lot of visitors, consider a four-legged table with extension leaves so it won't normally take up a lot of room.

Coffee tables Coffee tables generally sit in front of couches, so the size of a table is somewhat determined by the size of the couch. A coffee table is typically 16 in. to 17 in. high—the same height as a typical couch seat. This makes the table high enough for easy drink placement or for flipping through books while sitting on the couch. The table is also low enough that it won't impede your view of the television.

A coffee table should be proportioned to its couch and allow easy access to the couch. It's generally safe to make the table 2 ft. or 3 ft. shorter than the couch. As for the depth of the table, 20 in. to 24 in. generally looks about right and provides plenty of surface for assembling jigsaw puzzles, playing board games, and even eating dinner.

End tables Because end tables usually flank a couch or sit next to a chair to support a reading lamp, they are typically about 27 in. high. This height also allows easy reach to the tabletop from a standing position for picking up books, coffee cups, keys, etc. Arthur Chapin's End Table (p. 32) is a good example of customization. It is 30 in. high, because its maker and owner was over 6 ft. tall. Although

an end table certainly doesn't need one, a close-at-hand drawer can be useful.

Hallway tables A hallway table typically holds items for display. Because of its usual location in hallways and entryways, this type of table needs to be fairly shallow to allow easy passage around it. The Hallway Table on p. 48 works well with an 11-in.-deep top. Because this table also serves as a parking place for small items, such as keys, it should be at least 28 in. high so that the top is within easy reach. A drawer can be a nice aesthetic touch and provide storage for small items.

Console tables Console tables are generally placed against a wall and are used to display photos or hold lamps. They tend to be designed more for looks than for function. As such, you have great flexibility in their design. A height of somewhere between 24 in. and 32 in. should serve in most cases, depending on what you plan to set on top. The depth of a console table depends largely on its location and overall proportions.

Work tables Tables designed for work vary widely in dimensions and features, which largely depend on the type of work to be performed. The height of the work surface is perhaps the most important feature. If you sit while you work, you would want the surface much lower, of course, than if you stand. They also tend to have many drawers to increase their functionality, like the Shaker Sewing Table (p. 64).

Sizing a table to its room

Tables need to fit comfortably—both aesthetically and functionally—in the rooms they occupy. As an extreme example, you wouldn't use a card table as a dining table in a palace ballroom. When designing a table for a specific location, ask yourself, "Does it look like it belongs there?" Then try to match the table's style and size to its surroundings.

When gauging size, it's important to factor in the amount of space that is needed around a table, particularly one that people eat or work at. For kitchen and dining tables, allow 36 in. to 44 in. behind each chair so it can be pushed back. For wheelchairs, allow 54 in. And don't forget that a kitchen is a work-

Typical Pedestal Tables

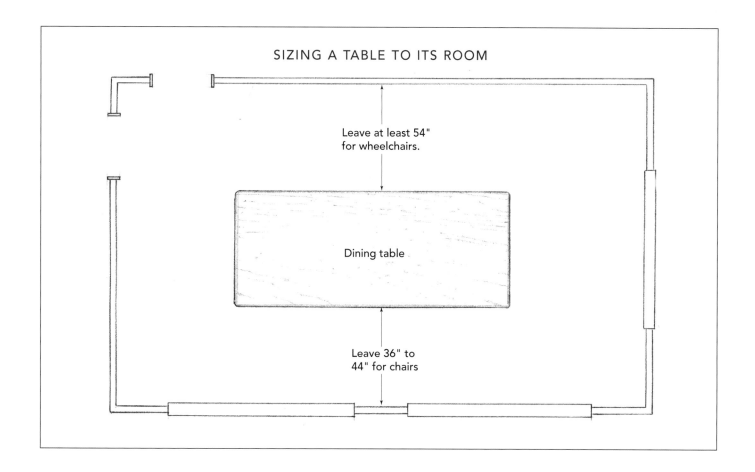

SIZING A TABLE TO ITS ROOM

Leave at least 54"
for wheelchairs.

Dining table

Leave 36" to
44" for chairs

room—you need space to move around while you cook.

These are all just guidelines, of course. Don't get hung up trying to gauge the exact room size and the precise dimensions for seating or anything else. You can probably eyeball a room for a good estimate of the appropriate table size.

One more thing: Don't forget to factor the size of doorways and hallways into your equations. It would be most unfortunate to build a kitchen table that won't fit through your kitchen door.

TOOLS AND EQUIPMENT

Sometimes we assume that every procedure requires the perfect tool and that without it we're helpless. In fact, with just a few good measuring tools, a good handsaw, a set of chisels, and a few planes, you can make just about anything out of wood. You can certainly make any table project in this book.

Tools, by themselves, don't make a piece of furniture better or worse in any important way; they just give you more options. And having fewer tools can be a blessing, because it can force you to develop new skills and discover new methods. After all, it doesn't take great expertise to feed a board into a surface planer and then rip it on a table saw. But to flatten it with a scrub plane and then rip with a handsaw—that takes some skill.

If you own a table saw and a few fundamental hand tools, you'll do fine. Work with what you have. If you don't have a finishing sander, use a scraper or a smoothing plane instead. No mortiser? Use a router or chop out the mortises with a chisel and mallet. No tenoning jig? Cut tenons with a handsaw. You'll find a lot of helpful step-by-step instruction on performing hand-tool work in this book.

A small set of basic hand tools will allow you to build any table in this book. They include smoothing and block planes, squares and rules, bench and mortising chisels, backsaws, scrapers, and sharpening stones.

To joint an edge at a right angle to a board's surface, a simple jig attached to a jointer plane ensures accuracy. There's no need to buy a jointer for such work.

MATERIALS

Wood is a unique material. Just by its very nature, it is beautiful. As Tage Frid says, you can take just about any scrap in your shop, plane it smooth, oil it, and you have a beautiful object. Wood is manufactured in a lot of forms, including plywood and other man-made boards. Whatever form you choose to use for your tables, design with the material in mind.

Solid wood

Solid wood is my favorite material for furniture, but using it requires serious forethought. Wood expands and contracts across the grain in response to seasonal changes in humidity. In the summer, it swells; in the winter, it shrinks because of the dry heat in a house. If a solid-wood panel is glued inside a frame, for example, it can crack when it shrinks. On the other hand, if it swells, it can explode the framework.

Waste is also a consideration when using solid wood. It's more expensive than man-made boards, and you can count on pitching at least 20 percent of any solid wood you buy.

Defects such as checks, cracks, and wane all need to be cut off and thrown away. Knots may or may not be considered defects, depending on whether you like the character they add to a piece of furniture. If you want to be choosy about grain composition—for disguising edge joints, matching curved grain to curved pieces, and so on—you're going to need even more wood. Personally, I think that woodworkers often get too precious about "the graphics of the grain."

Hardwood plywood

Hardwood plywood has some advantages over solid wood. It's less expensive and you'll generally incur less waste, provided you lay out your pieces judiciously. Also, wood movement is not an issue with plywood. It's constructed of veneers glued at right angles to each other, which restrains movement. Plywood typically comes in 4-ft. by 8-ft. sheets, saving you the trouble of edge gluing a lot of solid-wood boards to make a wide panel that you must then flatten, plane, and sand. Although hardwood plywood isn't generally available in a wide variety of woods, you can often find a decent selection at a good lumber dealer and even at some home centers. You can usually find it in thicknesses of ¼ in., ½ in., and ¾ in.

Plywood does have its disadvantages, of course. First of all, the thin face veneers are easy to damage and difficult to repair. Also, the plies on the edges of plywood panels show, which can be undesirable in many applications, unless you edge the panels with solid-wood strips or veneer. Rotary-cut plywood can display a distorted, almost un-realistic-looking figure, but you can often find plywood with sliced veneer faces that resemble solid wood. In spite of these drawbacks, plywood is an honest material and very useful for furniture making.

Medium-density fiberboard

Another man-made material that can be used in furniture making is medium-density fiberboard (MDF). A composition board made from wood chip fibers, MDF is extremely hard, flat, smooth, and stable. In furniture, it is primarily used as a substrate for veneering.

MDF is available in precise thicknesses of ¼ in., ½ in., ¾ in., and 1 in. Sheet sizes are generally 49 in. by 97 in.

MDF has several drawbacks. It is very heavy and is susceptible to water damage if left unfinished. And because it has no grain structure, large pieces can sag over time, so you need to make sure they are well supported structurally.

Veneer

Veneer is simply solid wood that has been sawed or sliced very thin. It is glued to a substrate to make components for furniture. Veneering—by nature a decorative art—has been around since early Egyptian times. Far from being a way to "falsify" solid wood, veneer fulfills some important needs. For one, it helps preserve many exotic woods that are becoming scarce these days and that are no longer available in solid form. For another, it's less expensive than using solid wood, making it a natural choice for tabletops, particularly large ones.

The basics of veneering are beyond the scope of this book, but there are many excellent articles on the subject in woodworking books and magazines (for example, see *The Veneering Book* by David Shath Square, The Taunton Press, 1995).

TABLETOP CONSTRUCTION

On the surface, making a large, wide, and flat tabletop seems a straightforward endeavor. However, getting it flat and keeping it flat for years to come can be difficult processes. Wood movement across a 36-in.-wide solid-wood tabletop can be substantial, from both internal stresses and seasonal moisture content changes. There are a number of ways to compensate and to keep your tabletop flat.

When choosing lumber, consider quarter-sawn stock. It moves substantially less than flatsawn stock and has much less tendency to warp. Flatsawn boards will tend to cup over time, flattening out the rings you see in the end grain. Quartersawn lumber does not do this.

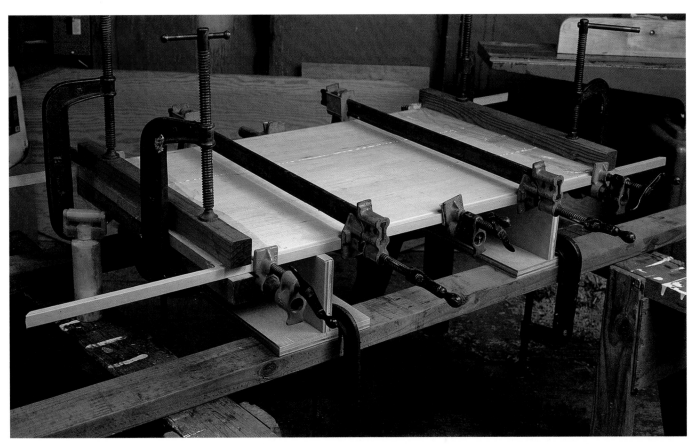

When edge-joining boards for panels, use hefty cauls on top and bottom, as shown, to ensure proper alignment. Wax on the surface will prevent the glue from sticking.

Dowels, splines, and biscuits (left to right) help align and reinforce edge joints for making panels or attaching panels to frames. They're also useful for joining frame members. Splines fit into long grooves in the mating members. Biscuits are football-shaped pieces that fit in arc-shaped slots.

Edge joints

A glued edge joint can be stronger than the wood around it. At the same time, it can be very difficult to align several long and wide boards in a glue-up. Without some help, the glue can act as a lubricant, allowing the boards to slide apart.

Dowels are an old way of aligning and attaching boards, although they do not add much strength because their effective glue surface is very small. Splines and biscuits are more commonly used. Splines insert into long grooves in the mating members. Biscuits are football-shaped pieces of compressed wood that fit in arc-shaped slots cut by a biscuit joiner.

My preferred method of board alignment, though, is much simpler. I simply sprinkle a few grains of sand at the ends of each board right before I clamp them together. The sand presses into the edges and keeps the boards from sliding apart.

End treatments

A good way to tame warping boards in a wide tabletop is to apply breadboard ends. The end will not cup or bow in the same way that the top will, so they can effectively cancel out their respective movements. Because the breadboards are attached across the grain, there are special joinery considerations to keep in mind.

Design-wise, breadboard ends can be nothing more than a board applied to the ends of the top to cover the end grain. At the same time, they offer design opportunities: You can make them thicker than the top or add details to the joint, such as pegs.

TABLE JOINERY

Tables—unlike wall cabinets, blanket chests, and many other pieces of furniture—are subject to a lot of abuse. We are always doing something on top of tables and moving them around. Without strong joints, parts can rack, loosen, and eventually fall apart. Because of this, you'll find that well-made tables incorporate mechanically strong, well-fit joints that are appropriate for their applications. Let's take a look at the joints used in the tables in this book.

Mortise-and-tenon joints

Probably the best joint for connecting table legs to aprons, the mortise-and-tenon joint is mechanically very strong. It provides a lot of long-grain to long-grain glue surface and is an excellent joint when resistance to racking is needed. The joint often includes a haunched tenon. The haunch allows more meat at the top end of the mortised member, while preventing the entire width of the tenoned member from twisting out of line.

Tip: After you glue up a top, always wait at least a day before sanding. Moisture in the glue can wick into the wood and make it swell temporarily.

BREADBOARD ENDS

To reduce warping across the grain on wide tabletops, you can attach a breadboard end. Dont' forget to consider wood movement when choosing a joint that goes across the grain. Never simply glue a breadboard end to a solid-wood panel.

Splined

Tongue and groove

Dovetailed

There are several variations on the basic mortise-and-tenon joint. Two that you'll find in this book are floating tenons and tusk tenons. A floating tenon, also called a loose tenon, is simply a length of wood glued into two mating mortises. The joint is just as strong as a typical mortise-and-tenon joint but is easier to make, because you don't have to saw a tenon on the end of one of the joint members. A tusk tenon is a knockdown joint that allows you to take frame members apart. A wedge inserted into the projecting end of a through tenon holds the joint together. It's a great joint for fastening the beam to the trestles on a knockdown trestle table.

Dovetails

A dovetail is another mechanically strong joint. A dovetail's primary strength lies in its angle of capture, which prevents the joint from pulling apart in one direction. Dovetails are commonly used to hold drawer corners together. Through dovetails are the easiest to make and are often used on the back of a drawer and on the front of a drawer box, if a false drawer front is to be attached. Half-blind dovetails are used at the front of a drawer to hide the joint.

Dovetails can also serve as frame joints, as when connecting a rail to a leg. A sliding dovetail joint can be used to attach a panel, such as a tabletop, to a long frame member.

Tabletop fasteners

Because solid-wood tabletops must be allowed to expand and contract, woodworkers have developed different ways of attaching tops to bases. One choice is to make wooden button blocks that fit into a groove in the apron and are screwed into the top. Commercially available S-shaped metal fasteners attach in the same manner. Another type of commercial metal fastener, shaped like a figure 8, is screwed in at an angle to both the apron and the top, allowing the top to move.

There are a couple of alternatives to using fasteners: One is to use a sliding dovetail joint, which is glued only at one end, as in the Danish Farmer's Trestle Table (p. 152). The other method is a bit more unusual. You make the base itself flexible, like the loosely half-lapped rails in the Oval Coffee Table (p. 182).

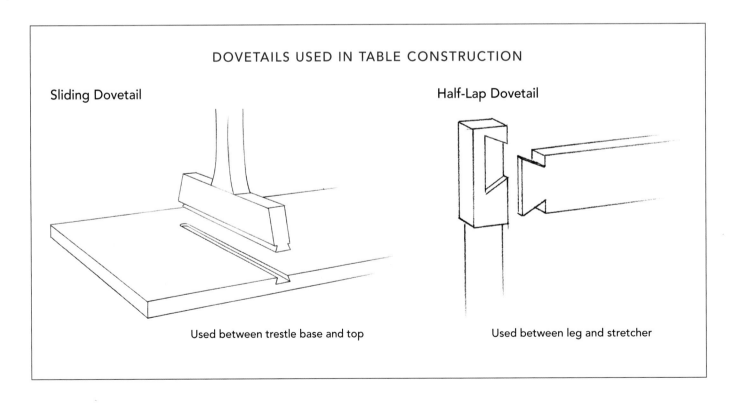

DOVETAILS USED IN TABLE CONSTRUCTION

Sliding Dovetail

Half-Lap Dovetail

Used between trestle base and top

Used between leg and stretcher

Typical Mortise-and-Tenon Joints

The strongest joint for connecting aprons to legs is the mortise and tenon.

BASIC MORTISE AND TENON

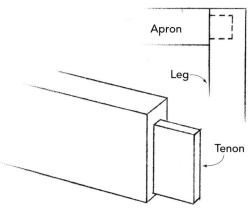

Apron

Leg

Tenon

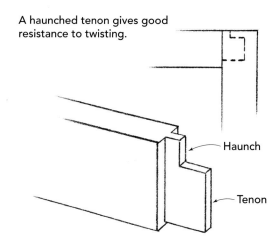

A haunched tenon gives good resistance to twisting.

Haunch

Tenon

A mitered haunch tenon is hidden from view on the edge.

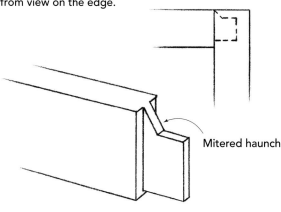

Mitered haunch

APRON AND LEG INTERSECTION

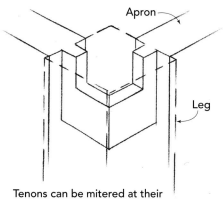

Apron

Leg

Tenons can be mitered at their ends to prevent interference.

Top View

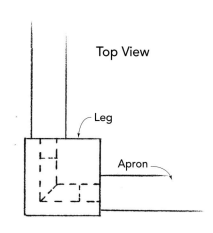

Leg

Apron

A floating tenon is a simple joint to make.

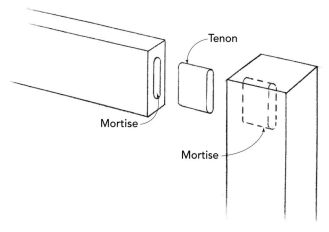

Tenon

Mortise

Mortise

Attaching Table Tops

**Pocket Holes
and Screws**
This joint is most
appropriate for
small tables. The
screws hold well but
do not allow
for much cross-
grain movement.

**Chiseled
Pocket Holes**
The holes for this
joint can be made
quickly with a sharp
chisel instead of
with a pocket hole
jig. Use this joint
only on small tables.

Screw Blocks
Blocks glued to the
apron and screwed
to the top make a
secure connection.
For wide tops, slot
the screws' pilot
holes to allow for
wood movement.

Button Blocks
These blocks are attached to the top and have tongues that fit into grooves in the apron; they allow for a good deal of wood movement. To prevent their breaking, make sure their grain runs perpendicular to the rails.

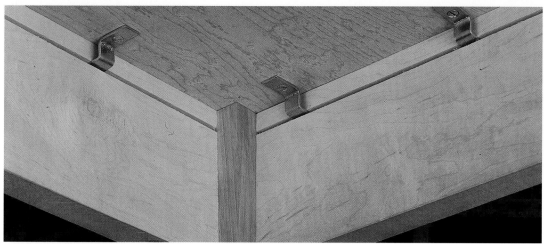

Metal Clips
Inexpensive and easy to install, metal clips screw to the top and fit into slots cut in the aprons. Although they work well, they look cheap.

Figure 8 Clips
These clips are more elegant than most metal clips. One half is mortised into the top of the apron and screwed in place. The other half is screwed into the underside of the top.

SHAKER CANDLE STAND

This pedestal table is one of my all-time favorite pieces of furniture. It is light, inexpensive to build, and unimposing. Originally designed to hold a candlestick, it can be used as a reading lamp table, a plant stand, an end table, or a bedside table.

I first saw a photograph of this candle stand in a 1940s book on Shaker furniture. I like this particular design—as opposed to the more common Champagne bottle style—because of its simplicity.

The candle stand shown here is a bit wider at the hips than the original—where the legs join the spindle—but it looks good from any angle.

Tiny changes in the proportions can make an enormous difference in the look of a piece like this. For example, the top must be slightly smaller in diameter than the span of the three legs. And the hub at the top of the spindle must be large enough to support the mounting ring but not too long, or it can ruin the fine taper of the spindle.

The shape and angle of the legs require the most attention. If the legs curve down from the spindle at the wrong angle, the piece will look either squatty or perched. The base looks most attractive if the bottom edge of each leg approximates a quarter-circle, as if the completed base could comfortably nestle on top of a sphere.

Shaker Candle Stand

THIS TABLE, originally designed by the Shakers to hold candles, can be used as a reading lamp table, a plant stand, an end table, or a bedside table. The top attaches with screws to a mounting ring that is joined to a turned tenon at the top of the post. Tenons on the legs slip into mortises that are routed into the post using a shopmade jig.

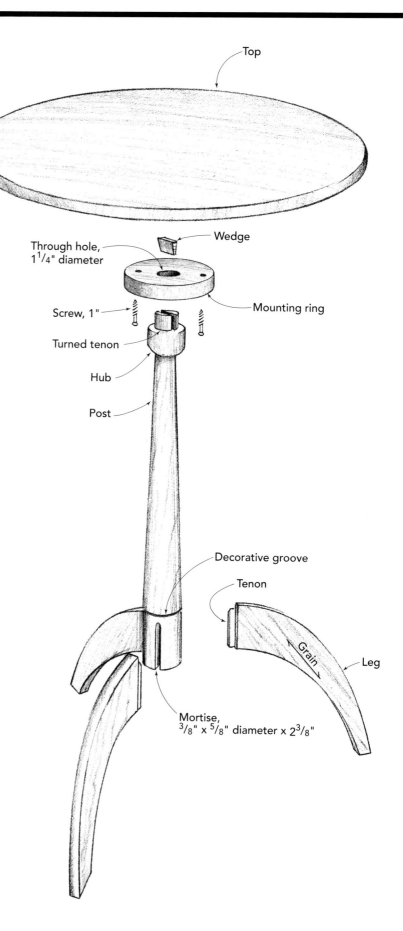

Top

Wedge

Through hole, 1$\frac{1}{4}$" diameter

Screw, 1"

Turned tenon

Mounting ring

Hub

Post

Decorative groove

Tenon

Grain

Leg

Mortise, $\frac{3}{8}$" x $\frac{5}{8}$" diameter x 2$\frac{3}{8}$"

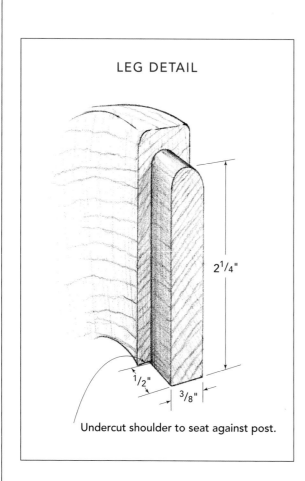

LEG DETAIL

2$\frac{1}{4}$"

$\frac{1}{2}$"

$\frac{3}{8}$"

Undercut shoulder to seat against post.

BUILDING THE TABLE STEP-BY-STEP

THE CANDLE STAND consists of three basic sections: the top, the post, and the legs. Its construction is fairly simple. As for tools, you'll need a lathe, a router, a saw for cutting curves, and a few hand tools. You'll also need to cobble up a simple jig for routing the leg mortises in the post. You can select any type of wood you like, but I find that this project is a good one for using up those smaller pieces of wood I can't bear to throw away. In fact, because I usually paint the tables, I'm able to use a variety of woods—often combining pine, cottonwood, poplar, aspen, hickory, or maple. I generally finish a candle stand with milk paint, followed by a coat or two of linseed oil.

MAKING THE TOP AND MOUNTING RING

Making the blank for the top

Whether you make the ⅝-in.-thick top from a single 14-in.-wide board or from several boards joined together, you'll need to flatten the top properly, because there are no aprons on this top to restrain it from warping. If possible, use quartersawn wood for its stability. If you don't have a jointer and planer, here's how to make and flatten the blank by hand.

1. Glue up the blank using ¾-in.-thick stock. Let the glue dry for 24 hours.
2. Flatten one side with a scrub plane, which has a convex cutting edge and is designed to remove stock quickly. Depending on the

CUT LIST FOR SHAKER CANDLE STAND

1	Top	14 in. diameter x ⅝ in.
1	Post	18 in. x 2 in. diameter
3	Legs	13 in. x 5 in. x ⅝ in.
1	Mounting ring	4 in. diameter x ⅝ in.

Photo A: Begin flattening the blank for the top by planing diagonally with a scrub plane to remove the high spots.

Photo B: After smoothing with a no. 5 jack plane, finish up planing the blank using a jointer plane, moving only in the direction of the grain.

amount of stock to be removed, the plane iron should project between $\frac{1}{16}$ in. and $\frac{1}{8}$ in.

3. Clamp the blank between your bench dogs and plane diagonally to the grain, first in one direction, then in the other (see **photo A** on p. 21). Flip the board upside down and try to rock it. If it lies flat, plane it diagonally again, but this time with a 14-in.-long no. 5 jack plane to remove the high spots. Use a good straightedge to check your progress. Finish up with a 22-in. to 24-in. jointer plane, cutting only in the direction of the grain (see **photo B**).

4. Set a marking gauge to $\frac{7}{8}$ in., the thickness of the top.

5. Referencing off of the flat side of the blank, mark a line all the way around the edge with the gauge.

6. Plane the blank to about $\frac{1}{32}$ in. shy of the line using the scrub plane. Follow up with the jack plane and jointer plane, as before, finishing up at your line. Handplaning a blank like this is not as time-consuming as it may sound. The secret is the scrub plane, which makes quick work of flattening even large panels.

Shaping the top

To shape the top, use a router and trammel. If you don't have a router trammel, make one from a piece of plywood (see "Shopmade Router Trammel").

1. Draw a 14-in.-diameter circle on the blank using trammel points or a compass.

2. To clamp the blank facedown to your bench without obstructing the travel of the router, drive a couple of screws through the corners into a large piece of scrap plywood, then clamp the plywood to your bench.

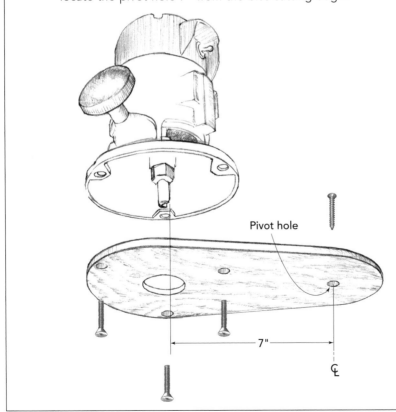

SHOPMADE ROUTER TRAMMEL

To cut circles with a router, make a trammel from ¼" thick plywood. To rout the 14" diameter candle stand top, locate the pivot hole 7" from the bit's cutting edge.

Pivot hole

7"

℄

Photo C: Cut out the circular top with a router and trammel.

3. Chuck a straight bit in your router, then locate and drill the pivot hole for the screw in the trammel 7 in. from the inner edge of the bit.

4. Place a screw through the pivot hole into the center of the blank—and through into the plywood to keep the top fastened down when it's freed from the blank. You can plug the screw hole afterward. Alternatively, you can attach the blank to the plywood with double-sided tape.

5. Set the router bit depth to ¼ in. and cut a complete pass, moving in a counterclockwise direction (see **photo C**). Complete the cutout by taking progressively deeper cuts until the top is freed from the blank.

6. Unscrew or unstick the top from the plywood and round over the top and bottom edges using a ¼-in. roundover bit (see **photo D**).

7. Finish up the top by plugging the center hole, if necessary, and sanding the top smooth.

Photo D: Rout both edges of the top using a ¼-in.-radius roundover bit.

Making the mounting ring

1. Mill a ¾-in.-thick blank for the mounting ring.

2. Use a compass to lay out the ring.

3. Bore a 1¼-in.-diameter hole through its center using a drill press.

4. Cut the circle out with a bandsaw or jigsaw. Smooth the edges with a spokeshave or rasp, rout the underside with a ¼-in.-radius roundover bit, and sand the ring.

MAKING THE POST

Turning the shape

If you laminate boards to create the thickness needed for the post, be sure to use the same species of wood, even if you plan on painting the piece. Dissimilar woods can expand and contract differently, creating a stepped joint line over time.

1. Cut your turning blank to about 3 in. by 3 in. and 22 in. long, squaring up the ends.

2. Mount it on the lathe and, using a roughing gouge, start turning at a slow speed until you knock the corners down.

3. Then crank up the speed and rough out the entire cylinder to a diameter of about 2¹⁄₁₆ in. (see **photo E**).

4. Switch to a skew chisel and smooth down the last 4 in. or so at each end to a 2-in. diameter. Be particularly careful to create a straight profile on the lower section of the post where the legs attach.

5. With the lathe off, mark out the reference points for the finished post (see "Post Dimensions"). Reference your layout from the center of the blank so that you're left with about an extra inch of material at each end. Turn the lathe back on and touch the pencil to each mark to extend it all the way around the cylinder.

6. Turn the round tenon. I use a skew chisel to cut the tenon, checking its diameter with calipers until it is exactly 1¼ in.

7. Still using the skew chisel, I then cut the ¹⁄₁₆-in.-deep, decorative groove 2⅜ in. up from the mark at the bottom of the post.

Photo E: Begin shaping the post with a roughing gouge, turning the blank to a 2¹⁄₁₆-in.-diameter cylinder.

POST DIMENSIONS

Reference points

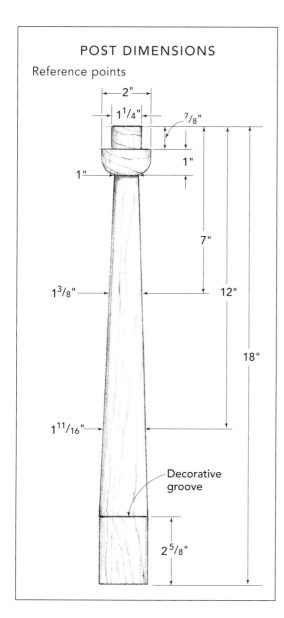

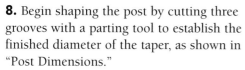

8. Begin shaping the post by cutting three grooves with a parting tool to establish the finished diameter of the taper, as shown in "Post Dimensions."

9. Check the depth of cut with calipers until you've nearly reached the finished diameter at each point. Turn the taper with a roughing gouge, stopping when you've reached the bottom of your reference grooves.

10. Then smooth the taper with a skew chisel (see **photo F**).

11. To finish up, round the bottom of the hub and sand the post. V-cut the ends of the

Photo F: After roughing out the taper with a gouge, smooth it with a skew chisel.

Photo G: Part the post from the blank, then saw off any remaining nubs.

Photo H: I use two gauges to help set up for mortising. The bevel-edged board sitting on the wall of the jig helps locate the mortise mark on the post at top dead center. The slotted jig resting on the router base quickly sets the proper distance between bit and edge guide.

post to part it from the blank (see **photo G** on p. 25).

12. Saw off any remaining nub.

Routing the leg mortises

Traditionally, a sliding dovetail joint was used to attach the legs to the post on candle stand tables like this one. This piece, however, is so light and designed to hold so little weight that a sliding dovetail is unnecessary. Instead, I use a mortise-and-tenon joint, which is easier to make and plenty strong for this application. I cut the mortises in the post using a plunge router and cradle jig.

1. To mortise the post, first build a jig as shown in "Post Mortising Jig." If you plan on making more than one of these tables, I advise making the two gauges shown, because they make the setup quick and accurate (see **photo H**).

2. Mark the mortises on the post, equally spaced one third of the circumference apart. For a neat trick on how to do this, see "Measuring around a Post."

3. Mount the post in the jig. Position the first mortise mark at top dead center. Set your router edge guide, then attach a stop block to stop the cut ⅛ in. below the decorative groove. If you're using a plunge router, set its depth stop for a ⅝-in.-deep mortise.

4. Rout the mortises. I begin with a full-depth plunge cut at the end of a mortise, which creates a clean mortise shoulder.

MEASURING AROUND A POST

Here's a trick for spacing the mortises equally around the post: Wrap a piece of masking tape around the lower section of the post, then make a mark on the tape where it overlaps itself. Remove the tape and divide the distance between the marks into three equal sections. (Each should be about 2⅛ in.) Rewrap the tape around the post and extend the tape markings onto it.

Post Mortising Jig

THIS JIG SECURES the candle stand's post in a cradle while the router rides on top of the jig's walls to cut each leg mortise. To set up the jig, clamp the post between the V-block and the cradle, with the mortise reference mark at top dead center. Set your router edge guide, position the bit to stop 1/8" below the decorative groove, and then screw a stop block to the jig.

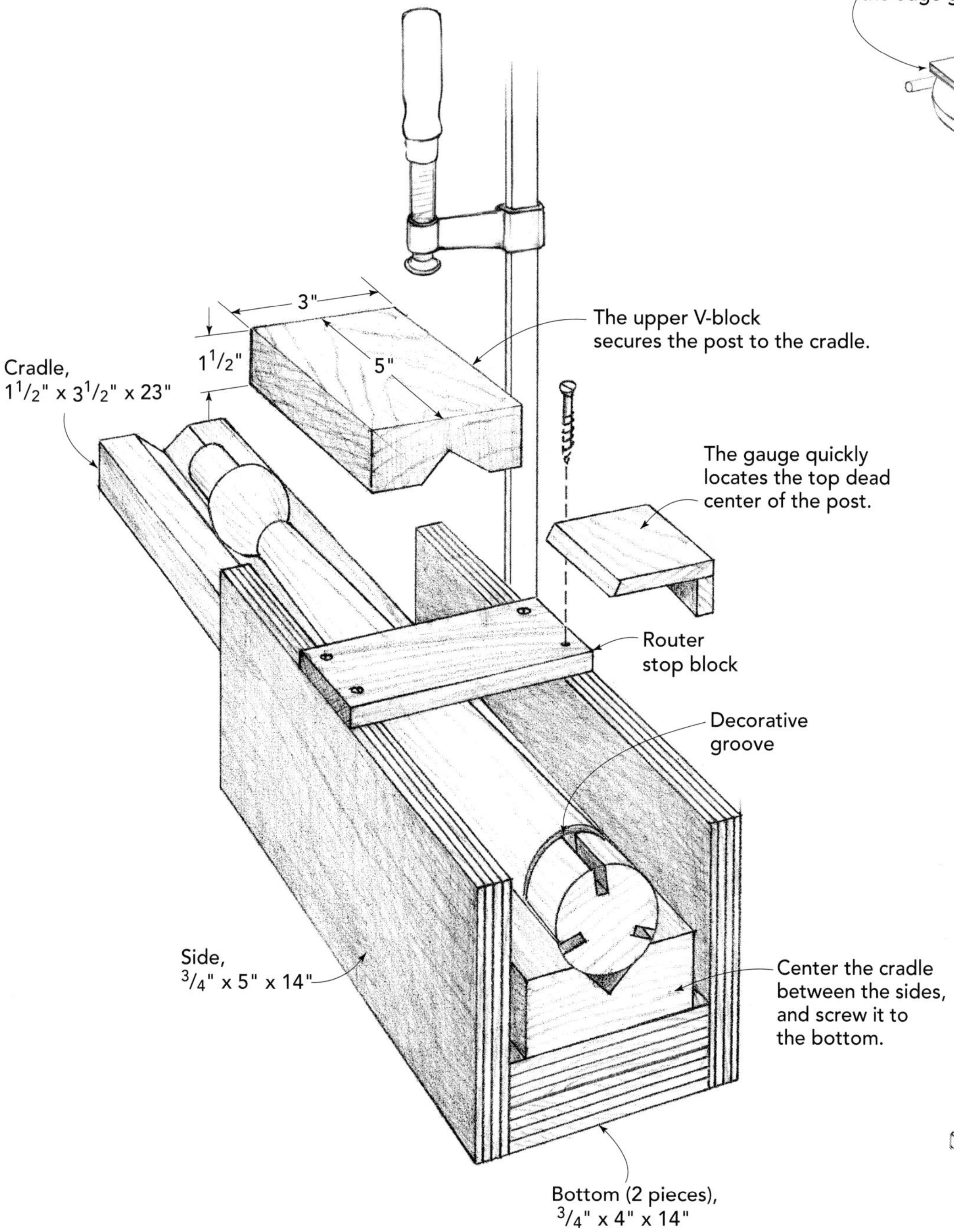

SETTING EDGE GUIDE

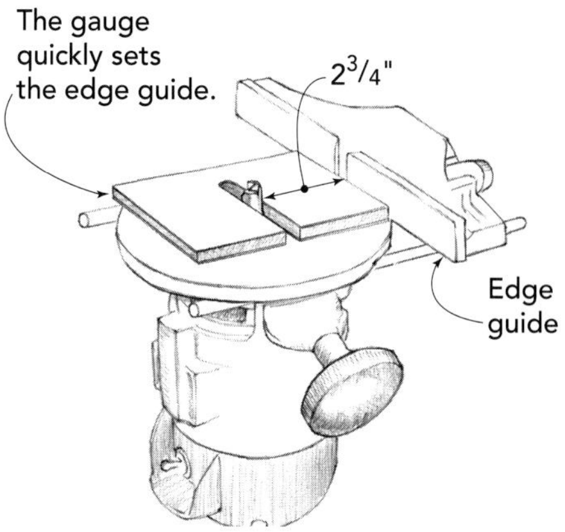

The gauge quickly sets the edge guide.

2³/₄"

Edge guide

3"

1¹/₂"

5"

The upper V-block secures the post to the cradle.

Cradle, 1¹/₂" x 3¹/₂" x 23"

The gauge quickly locates the top dead center of the post.

Router stop block

END VIEW

5/₈"

Decorative groove

Side, ³/₄" x 5" x 14"

Center the cradle between the sides, and screw it to the bottom.

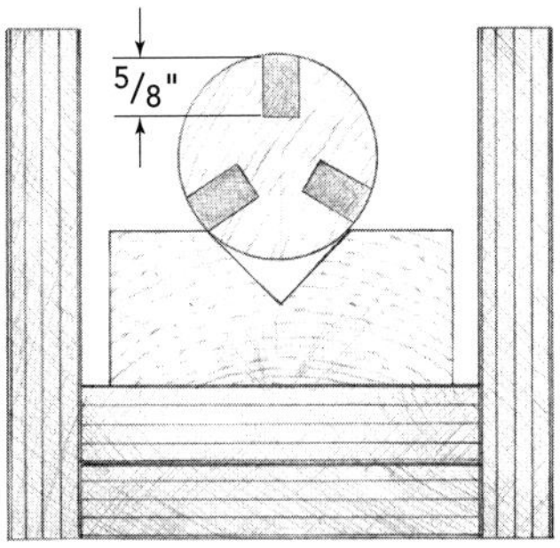

SIDE VIEW

Bottom (2 pieces), ³/₄" x 4" x 14"

2³/₄"

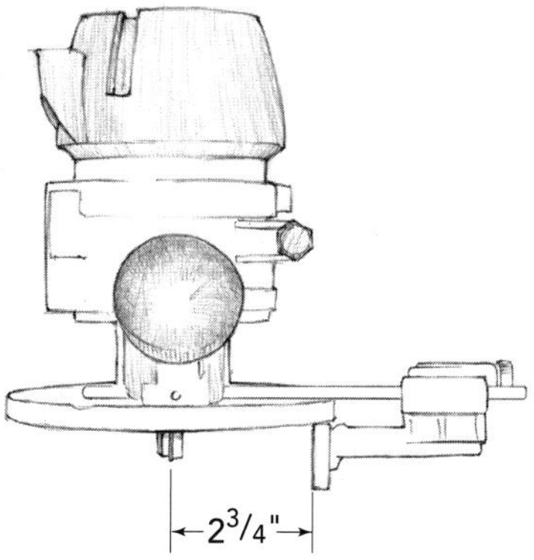

Photo I: With the post clamped securely in the jig, cut each mortise in a series of ¼-in.-deep passes. Begin at the end of the post.

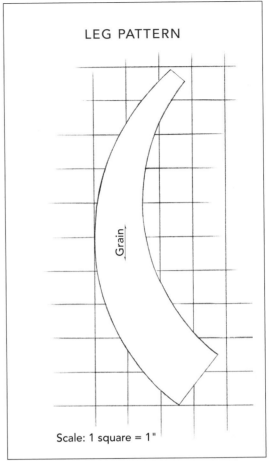

LEG PATTERN

Grain

Scale: 1 square = 1"

5. Complete the mortise by taking a series of ¼-in.-deep passes until you've reached the final mortise depth of ⅜ in. Be sure to begin the cut at the bottom of the post (see **photo I**).

MAKING THE LEGS

Sawing the shape

1. Start by making a ¼-in.-thick plywood template of the leg shape shown in "Leg Pattern."
2. After cutting the template to shape, smooth its edges carefully, then use the template to trace the leg pattern onto ⅜-in.-thick stock. Be sure to orient the grain to minimize the areas of weak, short grain.

3. Cut out the legs using a bandsaw, jigsaw, or scroll bowsaw (see **photo J**). Go slowly and keep the blade just off the line. Afterward, clean up any irregularities in the curve with a spokeshave or rasp.

Cutting the tenons

There are a lot of ways to make tenons, including cutting them with a table saw, a handsaw, or a router. You can also use a fillister plane, which is simply a rabbet plane with a fence and a front sole that adjusts up and down. I find that a fillister plane makes quick work of cutting these tenons, because there is so little material to remove. Here's how to use it to cut the leg tenons.

1. Set a cutting gauge to ½ in. wide, then mark the tenon shoulder lines on the sides and top edge of each leg.

2. Deepen the lines with a utility knife or chisel.

3. Set the fillister plane fence for a ½-in.-wide cut and adjust the front sole to a depth of ³⁄₃₂ in. or slightly less.

4. Clamp each leg flat on the bench and plane its tenon cheeks until the plane bottoms out against its front sole. If you set your plane correctly, your tenon should end up a bit too fat, which is what you want for right now. You'll fine-tune each tenon later when fitting it to its mortise.

5. While cutting, take care to keep the plane flat on the workpiece so that each tenon cheek ends up parallel to the sides of the leg. **Photo K** shows a tenon ready for final fitting to its mortise.

6. Test-fit each tenon in its mortise. It should be a bit oversize at first. (If it's too loose, you can glue veneer onto the cheeks to build it up.)

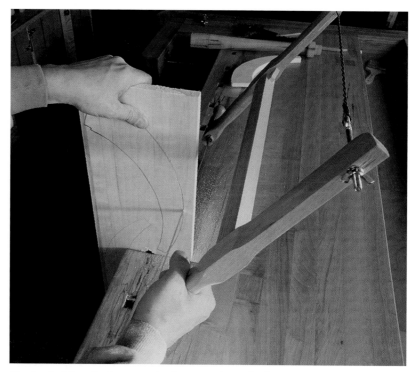

Photo J: After laying out the legs on ⅝-in.-thick stock, cut out the shapes using a bandsaw, jigsaw, or scroll bowsaw (shown).

Photo K: After initial cutting of the tenon with the fillister plane, shown here, the joint is ready for final trimming with a rabbet plane.

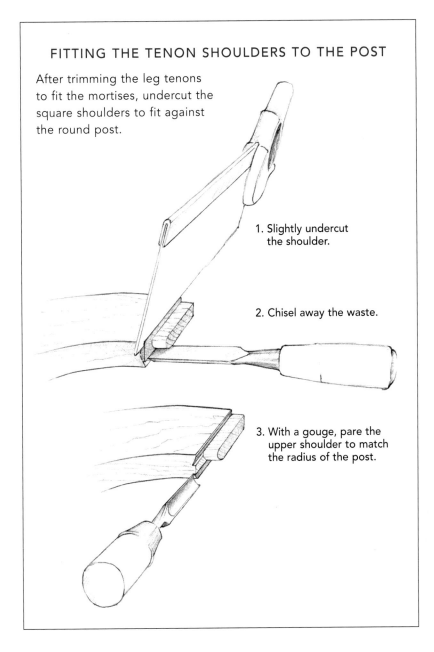

FITTING THE TENON SHOULDERS TO THE POST

After trimming the leg tenons to fit the mortises, undercut the square shoulders to fit against the round post.

1. Slightly undercut the shoulder.

2. Chisel away the waste.

3. With a gouge, pare the upper shoulder to match the radius of the post.

Fitting the tenon shoulders to the post

The final step in the leg joinery involves back cutting the square tenon shoulders so they'll fit tightly against the round post.

1. Saw each shoulder back at a slight angle (see "Fitting the Tenon Shoulders to the Post").

2. After chiseling out the waste, use a gouge to contour the top shoulder to match the post.

3. Finish up the legs by cutting a ¼-in.-radius roundover on all of the edges. Then finish-sand them.

ASSEMBLY AND FINISHING

Attaching the legs

To attach the legs properly, you'll need a flat, level surface.

1. Insert the legs into the post and stand the assembly upright on the surface. With a torpedo level resting on top of the hub for reference, adjust the legs up and down in their mortises until the post is plumb in all directions.

2. Draw a witness mark across each joint to register its position.

3. Remove the legs, brush glue in the mortises and on the tenons, and reassemble the joints, realigning the witness marks. Set the assembly aside upside down to dry.

Attaching the mounting ring to the post

1. Drill two ⅛-in.-diameter holes about ½ in. in from opposite edges of the mounting ring. Countersink them on the underside of the ring.

2. Saw a kerf in the top of the post tenon, cutting all the way down to the top of the hub.

3. Bandsaw a slim, tapered wedge to fit into the kerf.

7. Using a small rabbet plane, and making sure to keep it square to the tenon shoulder, take fine shavings off each cheek until the fit is snug. A good fit is very important here: The joint will have to hold its own during assembly, because clamping these legs is very difficult.

8. Saw ½ in. off of the top edge of the tenon and round it over with a rasp. The shape of the roundover isn't critical; there is already plenty of glue surface in this joint.

Photo L: Glue the mounting ring to the post tenon, orienting the wedge perpendicular to the grain of the ring. Apply glue to the wedge and kerf, then lightly tap the wedge in place.

Photo M: Attach the top with two 1-in.-long screws driven through the mounting ring. Orient the screws diagonally to the grain of the top to prevent wood movement problems.

4. Brush glue on the inside of the mounting ring hole and on the post tenon, then slip the ring onto the post. It's important to orient the kerf perpendicular to the grain of the mounting ring to reduce chances of the ring splitting when you drive in the wedge.

5. Squeeze glue into the kerf, spread some on the wedge, then lightly tap the wedge into place (see **photo L**).

6. After the glue dries, saw and plane the wedge flush to the tenon

Attaching the top

1. Center the post upside down on the underside of the tabletop. To minimize potential wood movement problems, I orient the screw holes in the mounting ring diagonal to the grain on the tabletop.

2. Attach the top with two 1-in.-long screws driven through the mounting ring holes (see **photo M**).

Finishing up

Do any necessary touch-up sanding, then apply your favorite finish. I like to use milk paint on these candle stands. Because you can vary the strength of the paint from translucent to opaque, you can either highlight the wood grain or hide it to cover mistakes or mismatched wood. After the paint dries, I apply two coats of boiled linseed oil, which deepens the color and provides some water resistance (see "Boiled Linseed Oil Finish" on p. 137).

END TABLE

This cherry end table was made by my father-in-law, Arthur Chapin, over 30 years ago. My wife grew up with it and loves it to this day. It's just the right height for a lamp, and the drawer is large enough to accommodate a fair amount of stuff.

Although very unpretentious, this table incorporates some neat little touches. Its solid-wood top sits on nicely tapered legs that are joined to the aprons with simple mortise-and-tenon joints. A dovetailed drawer slips between the two rails in front. The drawer runners—two rabbeted lengths of $1\frac{1}{32}$-in.-square stock—are a marvel of economy. They're easy to make, simple, and strong. The kickers, which keep the drawer from tipping as it's opened,

do double-duty as cleats for fastening the top. Slotted screw holes allow the top to expand and contract with changes in humidity.

I have to admit, I'm partially fond of this table because of the hands that made it and what Arthur taught me. I learned more from him than from any other woodworker or any school. He taught me the fine points of the craft: the importance of sharp tools and how to sharpen them. He showed me how to make good joints and how to use different kinds of woods.

His advice on finishing cherry applies to this table. "Don't use stain on cherry," he insists. "Daylight does the darkening, creating a rich, deep color that improves over the years."

End Table

THIS TABLE IS A MODEL of traditional simplicity. The aprons and rails attach to the legs with basic mortise-and-tenon joints. The drawer runners are simply rabbeted lengths of stock. The double-duty kickers attach the top and prevent the drawer from tipping. The false drawer front simplifies fitting the drawer.

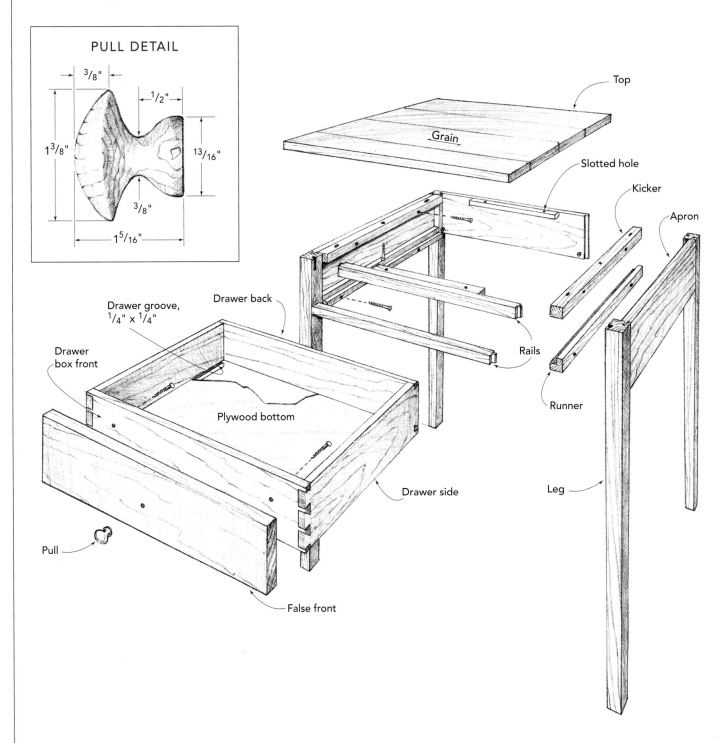

PULL DETAIL

3/8"

1/2"

1 3/8"

13/16"

3/8"

1 5/16"

Top

Grain

Slotted hole

Kicker

Apron

Drawer back

Drawer groove,
1/4" x 1/4"

Drawer
box front

Plywood bottom

Rails

Drawer side

Runner

Leg

Pull

False front

TOP VIEW

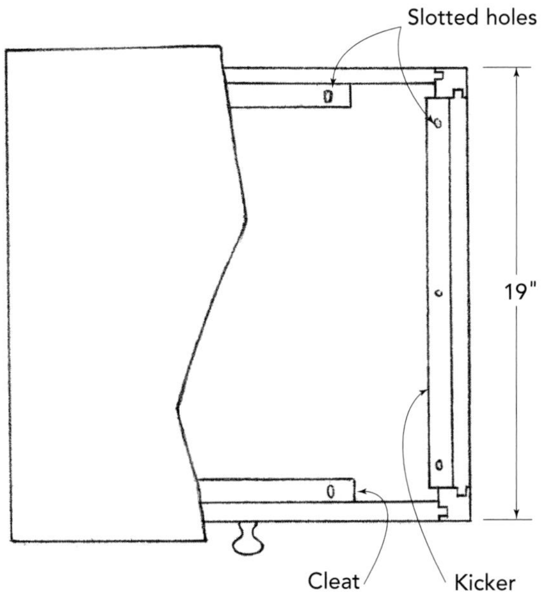
Slotted holes
19"
Cleat
Kicker

CUT LIST FOR END TABLE

Top		
1	Top	¾ in. x 20½ in. x 20½ in.
Carcase		
4	Legs	1⅜ in. x 1⅜ in. x 28½ in.
3	Aprons	¾ in. x 4¾ in. x 17 in.
2	Rails	¾ in. x 1 in. x 17 in.
2	Kickers	1 1/32 in. x 1 1/32 in. x 16¼ in.
2	Runners	1 1/32 in. x 1 1/32 in. x 16¼ in.
2	Cleats	¾ in. x 1 in. x 10 in.
Drawer		
1	Front	½ in. x 2¾ in. x 16¼ in.
1	Back	½ in. x 2¼ in. x 16¼ in.
2	Sides	½ in. x 2¾ in. x 16½ in.
1	Drawer bottom	¼ in. x 15¾ in. x 16¼ in.
1	False front	¾ in. x 2 11/16 in. x 16 3/16 in.

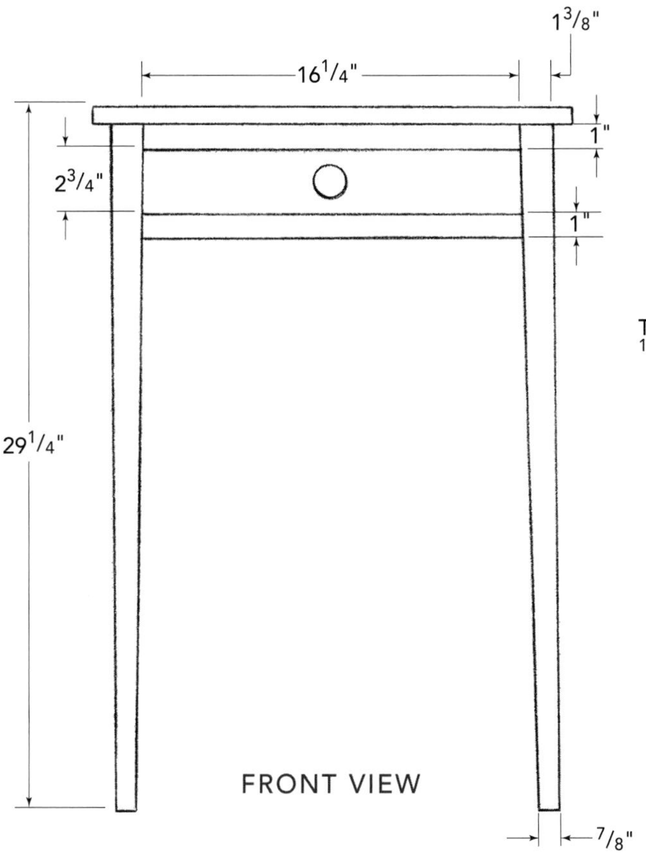
1 3/8"
16 1/4"
1"
2 3/4"
1"
29 1/4"
7/8"

FRONT VIEW

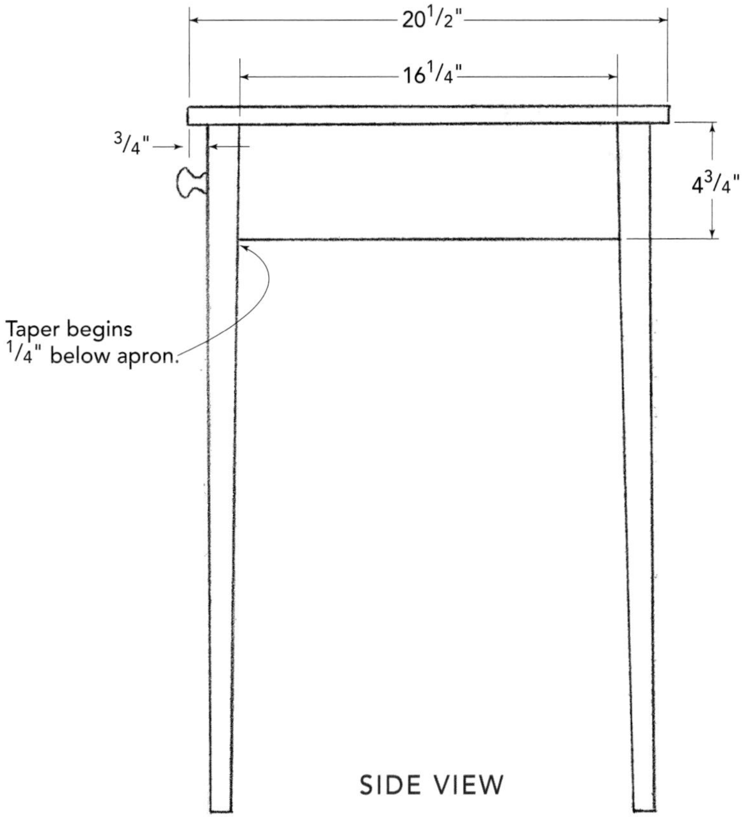
20 1/2"
16 1/4"
3/4"
4 3/4"
Taper begins
1/4" below apron.

SIDE VIEW

BUILDING THE TABLE STEP-BY-STEP

THE TABLE IS BUILT in three stages: the top, the carcase, and the drawer. It's important to make the drawer and runners last, because they are measured directly from the case. The drawer construction provides an excellent opportunity to practice making dovetail joints.

MAKING THE TOP

1. Mill enough ¾-in.-thick stock to make the top panel. Make the pieces slightly oversize in length and width for right now. You'll saw the panel to final length and width after gluing it up.

2. Joint the edges. If you use a handplane for this instead of a jointer, clamp two boards in the vise with mating edges side by side (see **photo A**). This way, any accidental angle will cancel itself out by opposing the angles of the two boards during glue-up.

3. Glue up the top, laying the boards across T-shaped clamping stands, which provide easy access to the clamps (see **photo B**).

4. When the glue dries, scrape any dried excess glue from the panel, then smooth it with a plane or cabinet scraper.

Tip: To keep freshly glued edges from slipping out of alignment under clamp pressure, sprinkle a few grains of coarse sand at the middle and ends of the joint before applying glue.

Photo A: To joint boards by hand, align two adjacent edges in the vise and plane them at the same time.

Photo B: Clamping stands allow easy access to the clamps when edge joining boards. The weight of the clamps on the top also helps pull the panel flat.

Photo C: A shop-made panel-cutting jig helps you squarely crosscut wide stock, such as the tabletop. The body of the jig is guided by a strip of wood that rides in the table saw's miter gauge slot.

5. Cut the top to final size. First rip it to width, then crosscut it to length on the table saw using a panel-cutting jig (see **photo C**).
6. Sand the top, rounding over the edges very slightly. Set it aside for now: You'll attach it after the table is completely built.

MAKING THE CARCASE

The carcase consists of three sets of similar components: the legs, the aprons and front rails, and the drawer runners and kickers. You'll need to work on the legs first, so you can fit the apron tenons into their mortises. Wait until the carcase is assembled to make and fit the drawer runners and kickers.

Tapering the legs

1. Dimension the leg stock to 1⅜ in. square, then cut all of the pieces to 28½ in. long. It's wise to cut material for one or two extra legs in case of mistakes. You can also use one of the extras to set up your tapering jig.

Photo D: Tapering the table legs is easy with a tapering jig. A tab at the operator end of the jig holds the work as you push it forward. As you near the end of the cut, hold the workpiece against the jig with a push stick.

2. Mark out the tapers on the two inside faces of one of the leg pieces, beginning 5 in. from one end. The taper decreases to ⅞ in. at the other end of the leg.

3. Taper the legs on the table saw using a jig (see **photo D** on p. 37). You could make your own tapering jig, but the commercial aluminum models cost only about 20 bucks, so why bother?

4. Plan your cutting sequence so that the second taper cut on each leg is made with a flat face of the leg lying on the saw table. Use a push stick and keep your eye on the blade. I like to shut the saw off to set up for each successive cut.

Photo E: Using a mortising gauge is a fast and accurate way to mark out the leg mortises.

5. Mount the leg in the jig, adjusting the jig's angle until the marked taper line is parallel to the rip fence. Then set the fence the proper distance from the blade to make your cut.

6. Saw the tapers about ½₂ in. fat, then plane them smooth afterward.

Mortising the legs

You can rout the mortises if you prefer, but the simple ⅜-in.-wide by ⅜-in.-deep mortises in these substantial legs can be easily chopped out by hand without fear of splitting the legs. Cutting mortises by hand isn't difficult, but it requires attention to technique. For a well-fitting, square joint, it's critical that you cut the mortise walls square to the face of the workpiece. But don't worry, that's something you eventually develop a feel for.

1. Lay out the mortises using a mortising gauge (see **photo E**). Adjust the gauge cutters so they're ⅜ in. apart and ³⁄₁₆ in. from the gauge fence. When marking the mortises, register the fence against the outside faces of the legs. Remember that one face of each front leg will get two short mortises for the rails.

2. Begin by selecting a mortising chisel that exactly matches the width of your mortise, which is ⅜ in. here. Place the chisel carefully between the mortise wall lines, orienting the sides of the blade square to the workpiece. If a mortise is near the edge of a workpiece, clamp it near the edge of your bench, to provide a sight reference.

3. Chop a series of V-cuts as deep as the chisel will comfortably go. Work outward from the center of the mortise (see **photo F**).

4. When you reach the end of the mortise, chop it square, staying about ⅛ in. away from your layout line for right now.

5. Clean out the chips using a swan-neck chisel (see **photo G**).

6. Repeat these steps until you've reached the bottom of the mortise.

7. Finish up by cutting the ends of the mortise square at your layout lines.

Making the aprons

1. Mill the ¾-in.-thick stock for the aprons and rails, and cut the pieces to their finished lengths and widths.

2. Use a marking gauge to lay out the tenon shoulders on the apron and rail pieces. Then use a mortising gauge to lay out the ⅜-in.-thick tenons on the ends of the pieces (see **photo H** on p. 40).

3. Saw the apron and rail tenons. You can do this on the table saw or with a router, but I prefer to cut them by hand and then plane them to a perfect fit. I use a bowsaw, because I find that it cuts faster and more accurately than many backsaws (see **photo I** on p. 40).

4. Saw the tenon shoulders to remove the waste.

5. Plane the tenons to thickness with a rabbet plane (see **photo J** on p. 41). The correct fit is not so tight that you need to hammer the joint together but snug enough that you need to use some hand pressure.

Photo F: Use a mortising chisel and mallet to cut the leg mortises. Begin by making a series of V-cuts, moving outward from the center of the mortise toward the ends.

Photo G: Even up the depth of the mortise with a swan-neck chisel.

Photo H: Mark out the widths of the apron tenons using a mortising gauge adjusted for a ⅜-in. tenon.

Photo I: Although you could use a backsaw to cut the tenon shoulders, I prefer a bowsaw for its speed and accuracy.

Assembling the carcase

1. Dry-fit the carcase together to make sure everything fits well. This is also a good opportunity to rehearse your clamping procedure before doing the actual glue-up.

2. First glue the side aprons to the legs with yellow glue. Make sure that the legs don't cock out of alignment under clamping pressure, or it will be difficult to attach the back apron and front rails. Check the diagonals to make sure the assemblies are square and then let the glue dry.

3. Glue the back apron and front rails between the two side assemblies. Make sure that the rails are parallel and check the diagonals across the top to make sure the case is square. Angle the clamps slightly if necessary to pull the unit into square. Place the table on a known flat surface such as your table saw top to make sure it stands solidly.

Making and fitting the drawer runners and kickers

Now that the case is assembled, you can mark the drawer runners and kickers directly from

it. It's important that the runners and kickers
project slightly into the drawer opening (see
"Drawer Runners and Kickers").

1. Mill up the runners and kickers.

2. Cut the blanks slightly oversize, then hold
each one in position against the carcase to
mark its final length.

3. Place each piece in the carcase and mark
for the final thickness and rabbets, allowing
for the 1/32-in. projection into the drawer
opening.

4. Make the cleats that attach to the back
apron and upper front rail. The dimensions
on these aren't critical. Align them with the
top edges of the rail and apron and attach
them with screws or glue.

5. Attach the kickers, aligning them to the
top edge of the aprons, as shown. Use screws,
but not glue, in case you have to adjust
them later.

6. Drill and counterbore holes in the kickers
and cleats for attaching the top. Elongate the
front and rear holes by about 3/16 in. with a rat-
tail file to allow for movement of the top.

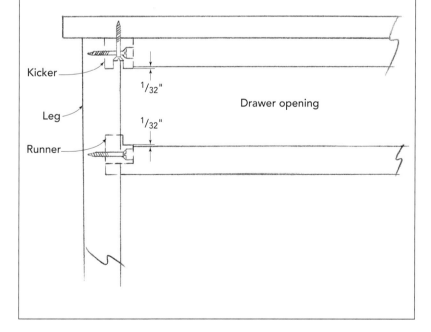

DRAWER RUNNERS AND KICKERS

When fitting the drawer runners and kickers, make sure they
project 1/32" into the drawer opening.

Kicker

1/32"

Leg

Drawer opening

1/32"

Runner

7. Attach the runners with only one screw in the front end. Align them parallel to the kickers and clamp their rear ends to the case sides for now. You'll do the final positioning and attachment later when you fit the drawer.

MAKING AND FITTING THE DRAWER

Arthur cut half-blind dovetails for his table drawer, but it's quite acceptable to use through dovetails with an applied front. This makes it easier to center the drawer front in the opening. The drawer sides, box front, and back are made of white pine; the false front is cherry. You'll build the drawer box to fit its opening exactly, then plane it to the final fit after assembly.

Dimensioning the parts

1. Thickness plane enough white pine to ½ in. to make the drawer sides, box front, and back.

2. Thickness plane stock for the false front to ¾ in. Make sure that all of the pieces are wider than the height of the drawer opening.

3. Rip the sides, drawer box front, and false front to width. To eliminate possible errors, mark the width of all of the pieces (which represents the drawer height) directly from the case. Rest one of the drawer sides on the bottom rail and mark where it meets the top of the drawer opening. Set your table saw fence to this distance.

4. Mark the length of the box front and back pieces. Cut one end of each piece square, then place it against the leg at one side of the drawer opening. Make a mark on each piece at the other end of the drawer opening and crosscut the pieces to length.

5. Mark the length of the false front directly from the drawer opening, subtract ¹⁄₁₆ in. from the length, and crosscut it to that dimension. Cut the drawer sides squarely to length.

6. Saw or rout a ¼-in. by ¼-in. groove into the drawer sides and front to accept the plywood

bottom. Then rip the drawer back to width, which is the distance from the top of a drawer side to the top of the bottom groove.

Cutting the dovetail joints

Hand cutting dovetails imparts a look that's impossible to duplicate with a router jig. It's also faster than setting up a jig if you have only one or two drawers to make. The following technique, which I learned from Frank Klausz, is a particularly efficient way to work. The front piece gets three tails; the narrow back needs only one. There's no need to space the tails evenly; just make sure that the

Photo K: Use a marking gauge set to the thickness of the drawer stock to establish the baseline for the pins and tails.

groove in the front piece runs through a tail, not a pin. Cut the pins first, then the tails.

1. Mark the top edges of all of your drawer parts to identify the front, back, and left and right sides. Also be sure to mark the inside face of each piece.

2. Set a cutting gauge to the thickness of your drawer stock plus ⅟₃₂ in. That builds in a total of ⅟₁₆ in. clearance for the drawer fit after you plane the projecting pins when the drawer assembly is complete.

3. Mark a line completely around the ends of each side piece, registering the gauge fence against the end (see **photo K**).

4. Mark a gauge line across the faces of the front and back pieces, but don't bother to mark across the edges. The gauge lines will serve as baselines when you cut the pins and tails.

5. Clamp the box front in your bench vise with the inside of the drawer facing you. Follow the steps in "Cutting the Pins," sawing down to the gauge line. There's no need to mark the angles, just saw by eye, cutting the angles somewhere between 8 and 12 degrees. It's important to hold the saw vertically for these cuts. When you're done, cut the pins on each end of the drawer back.

6. Chisel out the waste between the pins. Clamp the boards together on the bench with the narrow end of the pins facing up. Standing behind the work, place the chisel—with its back toward you—about ⅟₃₂ in. away from the gauge line in the waste area. Holding the chisel vertical and gripping it near the cutting edge, give it a couple of smart smacks with a mallet (see "Removing the Pin Waste" on p. 44). This beginning cut should drive the chisel backward to the gauge line. Make these initial cuts on all of the pin waste shoulders.

7. Angle the chisel away from you, holding it by its handle. Place the cutting edge on the waste area about halfway between the gauge

Cutting the Pins

VIEW FROM ABOVE

1. Cut the half pins at the ends.

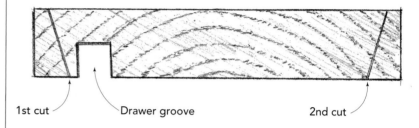

1st cut   Drawer groove   2nd cut

2. Cut the first side of the second pin.

Waste

3rd cut

3. Bisect the second and third cuts.

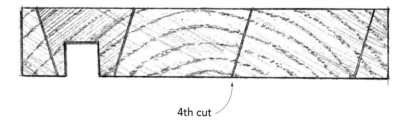

4th cut

4. Complete the pins.

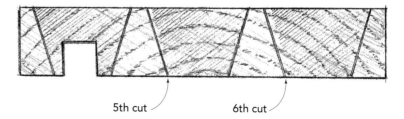

5th cut   6th cut

REMOVING THE PIN WASTE

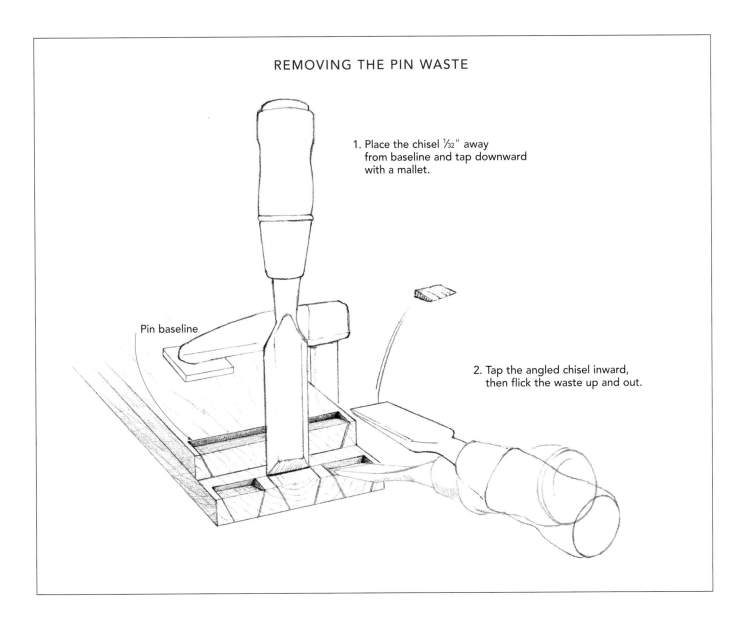

1. Place the chisel ¹⁄₃₂" away from baseline and tap downward with a mallet.

Pin baseline

2. Tap the angled chisel inward, then flick the waste up and out.

line and the end of the workpiece. With one tap of the mallet, slice down at an angle toward the end grain. Complete the motion by flicking the waste away with the chisel. Do this for all the pin waste areas.

8. Deepen the waste cuts by repeating the previous two steps—chopping downward at the gauge line, then making the backward angle cut. When making the gauge line cut, angle the chisel to follow the slope of the pins. When you're about halfway through both workpieces, flip them over, clamp them,

and repeat the process until the waste pieces have totally broken free.

9. Unclamp the work and clean up any fiber residue in the interior corners. Cut the pins on the other ends of the drawer front and back in the same fashion.

10. Lay the drawer sides on your bench with their insides facing up and their bottom edges next to each other. Stand the drawer front on end on top of its corresponding drawer side corner, aligning the edges, as shown in "Marking the Tails."

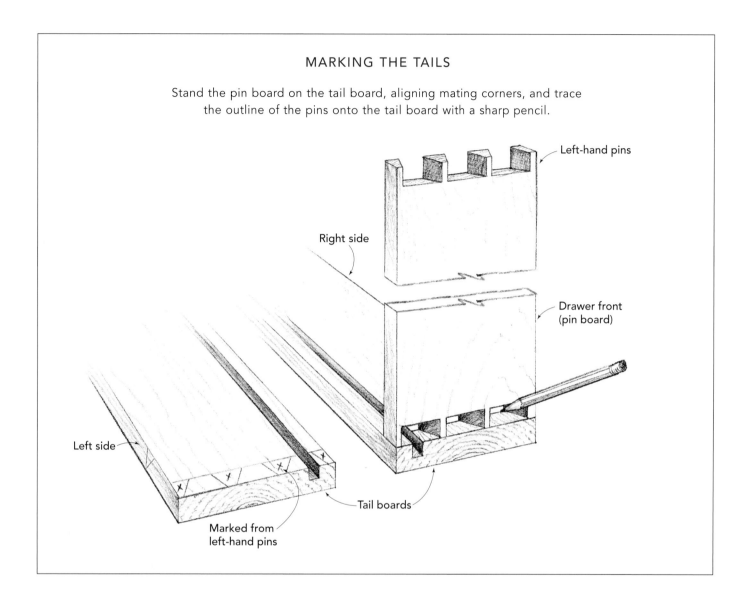

MARKING THE TAILS

Stand the pin board on the tail board, aligning mating corners, and trace the outline of the pins onto the tail board with a sharp pencil.

Left-hand pins

Right side

Drawer front (pin board)

Left side

Tail boards

Marked from left-hand pins

11. With a sharp pencil, transfer the shape of the pins onto the drawer side. Repeat for all corners of the drawer; mark the waste areas.
12. Clamp the drawer side upright in the vice with the pin outlines facing you. You may want to mark square lines across the end of the workpiece until you get the hang of cutting squarely by eye. Using a backsaw or bowsaw, cut down to the gauge line on the waste side of your pencil lines (see **photo L** on p. 46). When you've sawed all the tails, chisel

out the waste just like you did between the pins (see **photo M** on p. 46).

Assembling the drawer

1. Dry-fit the drawer, tapping the joints together, then measure for a snug-fitting drawer bottom. Make the bottom, ensuring that its corners are square; then set it aside.
2. Assemble the drawer box, spreading plenty of glue on all of the mating joint surfaces. A white polyvinyl acetate glue (like Elmer's) is a

Photo L: When cutting the tails, saw to the waste side of the lines you traced from the pins. Keep the sawblade square to the face of the stock.

Photo M: To make the initial baseline cuts on the tails, tap the chisel straight downward.

better choice than yellow glue for dovetails, because it's slower setting, allowing you more time to work. Tap the tails firmly into their pin sockets. A hardwood wedge placed on top of a tail between the pins makes a great hammer-tapping block. If your dovetails are snug, there's no need to clamp the drawer.

3. Stand the drawer on its front, and slip the drawer bottom into the side grooves, tapping it firmly into the groove in the drawer front. This should square up the drawer, but check the diagonals just to make sure. If the drawer is out of square, it won't fit properly. Nail the drawer bottom into the bottom edge of the drawer back.

4. Plane the pins flush to the drawer sides and the tails flush to the drawer front.

5. Plane the top and bottom edges of the drawer. To avoid tearout, plane around each corner in one smooth motion (see "Planing the Drawer-Box Edges Flush").

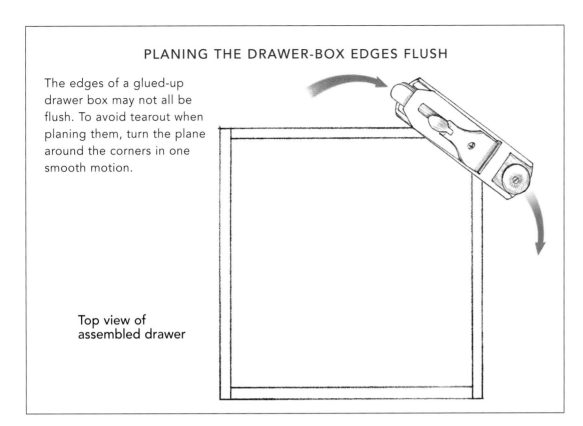

PLANING THE DRAWER-BOX EDGES FLUSH

The edges of a glued-up drawer box may not all be flush. To avoid tearout when planing them, turn the plane around the corners in one smooth motion.

Top view of assembled drawer

Fitting the drawer

1. With the rear end of the drawer runners still clamped to the case side, fit the drawer into its opening, planing it a bit if necessary. Ensure that the drawer rides level on both runners, adjusting them up or down, as needed. When the drawer operates smoothly, screw the rear of the runners to the case side.

2. Turn the drawer pull and screw it to the false drawer front from the inside face.

3. Next attach the false drawer front by first pushing the drawer box in ¾ in. from the front of the rails.

4. Center the box between the runners, shimming if necessary, then clamp the drawer sides to the case sides from above, making sure that the drawer is sitting solidly on its runners.

5. Test-fit the false front into the drawer opening. You should have about a ½₂-in. gap on each side. Plane the top and bottom edges to achieve the same gap.

6. Center the false front in its opening using shims and clamp it to the drawer box front. Attach it with screws from inside the drawer.

7. Install the drawer stops, which are simply screws driven into the back apron. This is the same technique used for the Hallway Table (see p. 48).

8. Adjust the screws in or out to align the false front flush to the rails.

FINISHING UP

1. Attach the top to the carcase, running screws through the cleats and drawer kickers.

2. Apply your favorite finish. I suggest a couple of coats of linseed oil, waxing it afterward if you want a glossier finish. But under no conditions stain the cherry. You do that and you're gonna have to answer to Arthur....

Hallway Table

This graceful, narrow oak table is designed to sit in a hallway, behind a sofa, or anywhere where depth of space is limited. I designed the table with more attention to form than to function. Although it's very strong, it looks as light and delicate as possible without appearing fragile. A piece of furniture like this is not really meant to hold heavy stuff, anyway. It's typically used as a landing place for car keys and as a pedestal for candles, greeting cards, and other miscellany. The drawers usually become a home to pencils, matches, catnip, and other bits of life's little accessories.

The design stems from a number of influences, including Shaker and Japanese. To some extent, it was also determined by the thin stock I had on hand. But the material resulted in a pleasing look. The ⅜-in.-thick top appears to rest lightly atop the 1-in.-square legs that taper to ⅝ in. at their feet. The breadboard ends, which cap tenons on the top, provide a traditional design element while restricting warpage.

The table is very strong because of its joinery. The apron tenons extend deeply into the leg mortises, creating a hearty mechanical joint with a lot of glue surface. The carcase also gains rigidity from its central dovetailed apron stretcher and from the drawer runners and kickers that extend from front to back.

Hallway Table

THIS DELICATE HALLWAY TABLE has roots in Japanese and Shaker design. The very thin top, only ⅜" thick, has breadboard ends that sit proud and are attached with dowels. The strong carcase is traditional, with mortise-and-tenon joints between the aprons and the legs and dovetailed stretchers between the aprons.

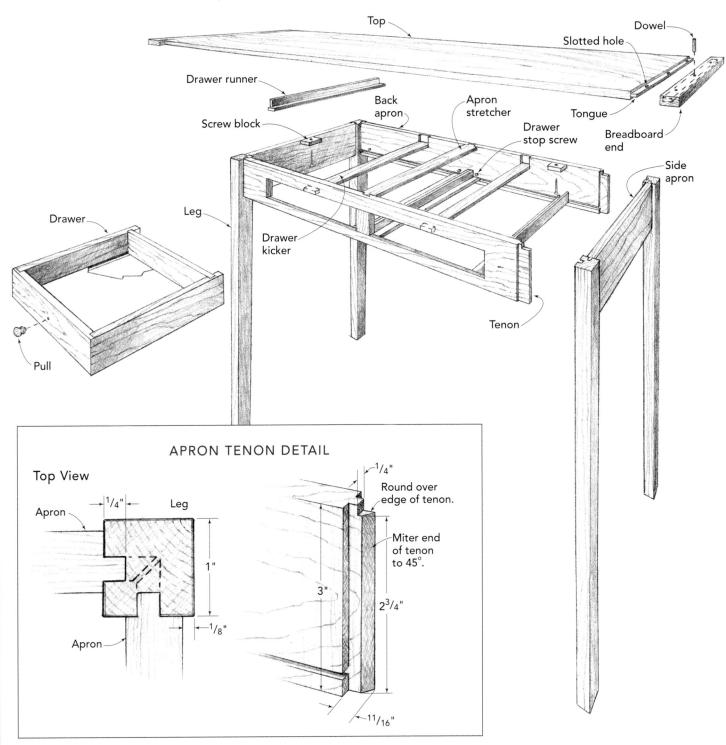

APRON TENON DETAIL

Top View

Apron

Leg

1/4"

Apron

1"

1/8"

Round over edge of tenon.

Miter end of tenon to 45°.

1/4"

3"

2 3/4"

11/16"

TOP VIEW

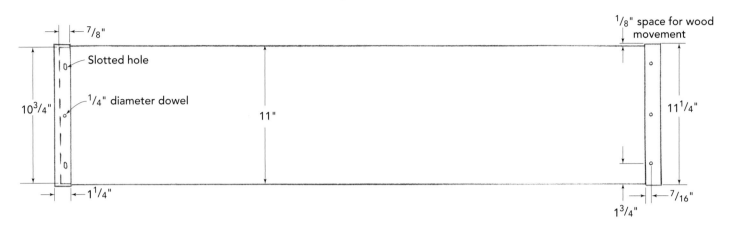

7/8"

Slotted hole

1/4" diameter dowel

10³/4"

11"

1/8" space for wood movement

11¹/4"

1¹/4"

1³/4"

7/16"

FRONT VIEW

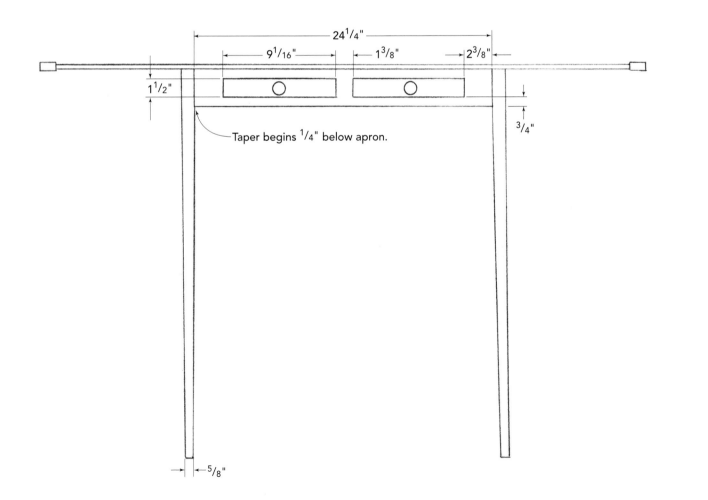

24¹/4"

9¹/16"

1³/8"

2³/8"

1¹/2"

3/4"

Taper begins ¹/4" below apron.

5/8"

BUILDING THE TABLE STEP-BY-STEP

CUT LIST FOR HALLWAY TABLE

Top		
1	Plank	3/8 in. x 11 in. x 48 1/4 in.
2	Breadboard ends	5/8 in. x 1 1/4 in. x 11 1/4 in.
Carcase		
4	Legs	1 in. x 1 in. x 30 3/4 in.
2	Aprons (front and back)	5/8 in. x 3 in. x 25 5/8 in. (including tenons)
2	Aprons (side)	5/8 in. x 3 in. x 9 3/8 in.
1	Apron stretcher	3/4 in. x 1 1/4 in. x 9 3/8 in.
4	Drawer runner bottoms	5/16 in. x 1 in. x 9 in.
4	Drawer runner sides	5/16 in. x 5/8 in. x 8 1/2 in.
2	Drawer kickers	5/16 in. x 1 in. x 8 3/4 in.
Drawers		
2	Fronts	5/16 in. x 1 1/2 in. x 9 in.
2	Backs	5/16 in. x 1 in. x 8 3/8 in.
4	Sides	5/16 in. x 1 1/2 in. x 8 3/4 in.
2	Bottoms	1/4 in. x 8 5/8 in. x 8 5/16 in.

THE TABLE BASICALLY consists of a top, a carcase, and the drawers. I generally make the top first. The carcase must be built before the drawers are made, because they are carefully fit to their openings. When making the carcase, you'll make and mortise the legs first and then make the aprons, fitting their tenons into the leg mortises.

MAKING THE TOP

Making the plank

If you're gluing up stock to get the width, you shouldn't use more than a board or two to make up the 11-in.-wide top.

1. Mill up a board or boards for a slightly oversize top—about 1 1/2 in. more in length and about 1/2 in. in width.
2. Thickness the boards to about 1/2 in. thick before joining them. You can thickness them

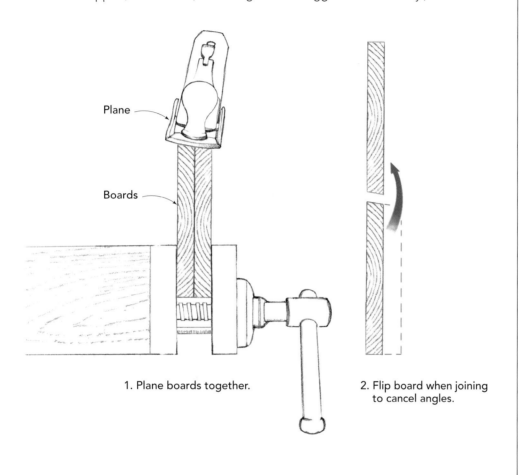

EDGE JOINTING BY HAND

When handplaning the mating edges of two boards to be edge joined, clamp both pieces together in a vice and plane them at the same time. That way, any unintended angle will cancel itself out when one board is flipped, as shown. (Note: Angles are exaggerated for clarity.)

Plane

Boards

1. Plane boards together.

2. Flip board when joining to cancel angles.

later with handplanes (see "Making the Blank for the Top" on p. 21) or by machine. If using a thickness planer, be sure to flatten one face first on a jointer. Otherwise, if the board is warped, it will simply spring back to its warped shape as it leaves the planer.

3. Joint the edges of the boards. You can use a jointer for this, but I find it easier to plane them by hand.

4. Clamp the boards together in the work-bench vise, with the mating edges flush to each other, and joint them both at once with a sharp jointer plane. This way, any unintended angle will cancel itself out when one of the boards is flipped (see "Edge Jointing by Hand").

5. Glue the boards together with yellow glue. Sprinkling a grain or two of coarse sand into

Photo A: Use a cutting gauge to mark the shoulders of the tongue. Then deepen the gauge line with a knife or series of chisel cuts to prevent tearout when planing the tongue.

SPRINGING A BOARD

When jointing the edges of boards before gluing them together, I like to add a final touch by "springing" the joint. I take a few light passes with the plane at the center of the board while holding the plane skewed. The resulting slight concavity ensures that the boards meet tightly at their ends when glued together. When you hold the boards up to a light, edges together, you will see a gap of about ⅟₆₄ in. at the center. You should be able to squeeze this joint shut using hand pressure, although you may not always be able to do this with thicker boards.

the glue near the ends and middle of the joint will keep the boards from creeping under clamp pressure.

6. Start clamping at the center and alternate the clamps—one over, next one under, etc. Make sure that the boards are flush at the glueline, but don't apply too much pressure; you don't want these thin boards to buckle.

7. After the glue has dried, plane the top to its final ⅜-in. thickness.

8. Rip and crosscut the top to final size, remembering to include the tenons in the length. Do any necessary smoothing now, because it will be nearly impossible to do so after attaching the breadboard ends.

Making and fitting the breadboard ends

The breadboard ends stiffen the top and prevent warping. To allow cross-grain movement of the top, the breadboards are left unglued. Instead, the joint is pinned with ¼-in.-diameter dowels, which fit through slotted holes in the tenon.

Photo B: After sawing the shoulder at the edge of the plank, cut the tongue with a fillister plane. Planing the tongue, rather than sawing or routing it, allows you to fine-tune its thickness for a perfect fit in its breadboard end groove.

Photo C: Dry-clamp the breadboard end onto the plank, then drill the dowel holes. The backer block clamped to the underside prevents exit tearout.

1. Plane and saw the breadboard ends to size.
2. Rout a ¼-in.-wide by ¹⁵⁄₁₆-in.-deep groove in one edge of each piece, stopping ¼ in. from each end. To provide a steady bearing surface for the router, I shim and wedge the workpiece into a jig that I made for routing mortises in narrow stock and use a router fence to guide it (see "Router Mortising Jig" on p. 147).
3. Set a cutting gauge to ⅞ in. and mark the tenon shoulders on each end of the table plank (see **photo A**). To prevent tearout when cutting the tenon, deepen the line with a knife cut or series of chisel cuts.
4. On each side of the end of the plank, cut ¹⁄₁₆-in.-deep rabbets to create the tenon. Planing the rabbets is faster and more accurate than sawing or routing them. I use a fillister

plane, which is a rabbet plane fitted with a fence, a depth stop, and a "nicker" for cutting the shoulder (see **photo B**). If you use a fence-less rabbet plane, guide it with a thick wooden straightedge clamped on the gauge line. As you plane, occasionally test the tenon's fit in its groove.
5. When the joint is comfortably snug, saw ¼ in. off the ends of the tenon to fit in the stopped groove. The ¼-in. step will also leave room for some cross-grain expansion of the top. Round over the ends of the tenon to match the radius of the groove.

Attaching the breadboard ends

1. Mark the dowel locations on the breadboard ends (see "Top View" on p. 51).

2. Clamp the breadboard ends in place, carefully centering them on the ends of the plank. Clamp the assembly to your benchtop to keep it from moving while you drill.

3. Drill the three dowel holes completely through each breadboard end and tenon (see **photo C** on p. 55).

4. Remove the breadboard ends and elongate the outermost holes in the tenons by about ³⁄₁₆ in. with a rat-tail file (see **photo D**).

5. Reattach the breadboard ends, spread just a dab of glue around the uppermost edge of each hole, and insert the dowels. Avoid dripping glue onto the tongue.

6. After the glue has dried, saw and chisel the dowels flush to the breadboard ends (see **photo E**).

Photo D: To accommodate cross-grain movement of the plank, elongate the outermost holes in the tongues.

Photo E: Pin the unglued breadboard ends to the plank with dowels sparingly glued into their holes. Trim them flush after the glue dries.

MAKING THE CARCASE

Shaping the legs

1. Rip, joint, and crosscut the blanks for the tapered legs. Make an extra blank for setting up your tapering jig.

2. Mark the taper on one face of your extra blank. The taper begins 3¼ in. from one end and diminishes to ⅝ in. at the other.

3. Saw the taper on the test blank. I use a tapering jig like the one I used for the End Table (see p. 37).

4. Mount the leg in the jig, adjusting the jig's angle until the marked taper line is parallel to the rip fence. Then set the fence the proper distance from the blade to make your cut. I saw the tapers about 1⁄64 in. fat, then plane them smooth afterward. Plan your cutting sequence so that the second taper cut on each leg is made with a flat face of the leg laying on the saw table. Use a push stick and keep your eye on the blade. I shut the saw off to set up for each successive cut.

5. After the tapering jig is properly set up, taper all of the legs.

6. Plane away the saw marks.

Mortising the legs

The leg mortises house the ¼-in.-thick, haunched apron tenons, which meet inside the legs. The aprons are set back ⅛ in. from the outside faces of the legs (see "Apron Tenon Detail" on p. 50).

1. Set the blade of a combination square to project ⅛ in. and mark the apron setback on the inside faces of each leg. This will prevent confusion when cutting the mortises.

2. Mark a pencil line across each joint face ¼ in. down from the top of the leg to establish the haunch spacing. Then mark a line 3 in. down from the top to define the end of each mortise.

3. Lay out the ¼-in.-wide mortise walls on one of the legs, locating the outer wall 5⁄16 in. from the outside faces of the legs. Because you'll be using the same router edge guide setting to cut all the mortises, there's no need to lay out the mortise walls on the other legs.

4. Wedge or clamp the marked leg into the same jig that you used for routing the groove in the breadboard ends. Set your router edge guide using the mortise wall marks and cut the first mortise. Rout the depth in increments of ¼ in. or less.

5. Rout the rest of the mortises, making sure that each pair in a leg meets inside in a neat corner.

Making the apron pieces

The aprons are identical in thickness, width, and tenon size, making tool setup very efficient. Make the two drawer openings by ripping the front apron blank into three pieces, crosscutting sections from the center piece, then gluing the pieces back together. This needs to be done before cutting all of the rails to final size.

1. Mill enough ⅝-in.-thick stock to make the aprons, leaving the pieces slightly oversize in length and width for right now. The blank for the front apron should be about 3½ in. wide.

2. Make the front apron by first ripping a 1½-in.-wide strip from the center of the blank. Then crosscut spacer blocks from the center strip into the sizes shown in "Front View" (see p. 51). To maintain grain continuity in the finished apron, mark and cut the blocks from the middle and ends of the center strip.

3. Joint the edges of the narrow top and bottom strips and carefully mark out the drawer opening spacing on them.

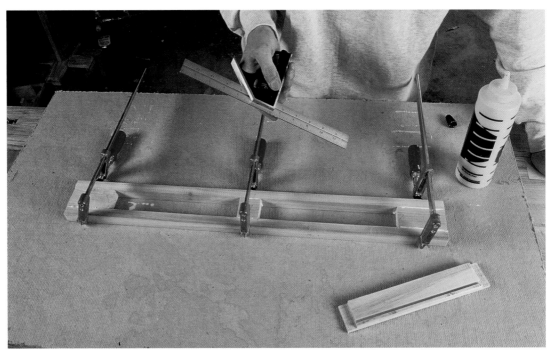

Photo F: To make the front apron, rip the blank into three strips, then cut out sections of the center strip to create the drawer openings. Glue the pieces back together, carefully measuring the openings.

4. Glue the pieces together, carefully aligning the spacer blocks to your reference marks to create the two 9 $\frac{1}{16}$-in.-wide drawer openings. Check the drawer opening spacing with a ruler before and after applying clamping pressure (see **photo F**). After the glue dries, scrape away any excess and plane the apron smooth.

5. Rip, joint, and crosscut all of the aprons to final size, remembering to include the tenon length. Mark all of the pieces for position using "The Triangle Marking System" on p. 78.

Cutting the apron joints

In addition to the tenons, the grooves for the drawer runners need to be cut before assembling the aprons to the legs. It's also easiest to make the notches for the drawer kickers and dovetailed stretcher rail before assembly.

1. Saw or rout the $\frac{5}{16}$-in.-wide by $\frac{1}{4}$-in.-deep grooves in the aprons for the drawer runners. Space the bottom edge of the groove $\frac{15}{32}$ in. away from the bottom edge of the apron (see "Drawer Runner and Kicker Attachment"). This will cause the $\frac{5}{16}$-in.-thick drawer runners to project $\frac{1}{32}$ in. into the drawer openings (see "Runners and Kickers").

2. Lay out and rout the $\frac{1}{8}$-in.-deep notches that house the ends of the drawer kickers. The notches in the front apron border the drawer opening. The rear notches border the top of the back rail.

3. Mill the apron stretcher to size and cut the dovetails on its ends. Each dovetail is $\frac{7}{16}$ in. long. Trace the outline of each tail onto the middle of its mating apron, then saw and chisel out the dovetail notches.

4. Lay out a tenon on the end of an apron. First, set a cutting gauge to $\frac{11}{16}$ in. and mark

DRAWER RUNNER AND KICKER ATTACHMENT

The drawer runners are tacked with finish nails into grooves milled into the front and back aprons. The kickers are tacked into notches in the aprons.

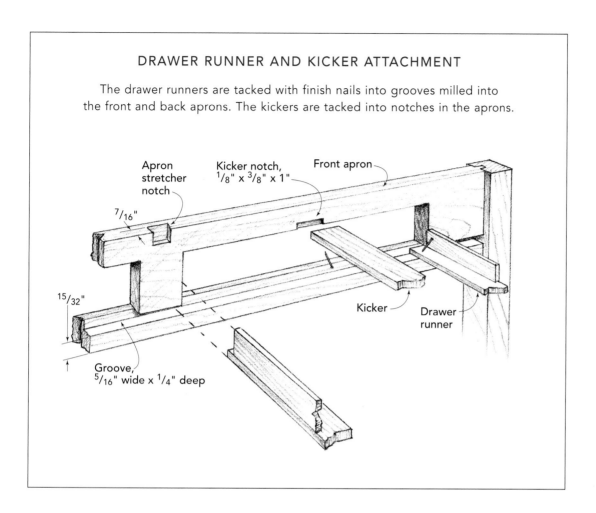

Apron stretcher notch

Kicker notch, 1/8" x 3/8" x 1"

Front apron

7/16"

15/32"

Groove, 5/16" wide x 1/4" deep

Kicker

Drawer runner

RUNNERS AND KICKERS

Fit drawer runners and kickers to project 1/32" into the drawer openings.

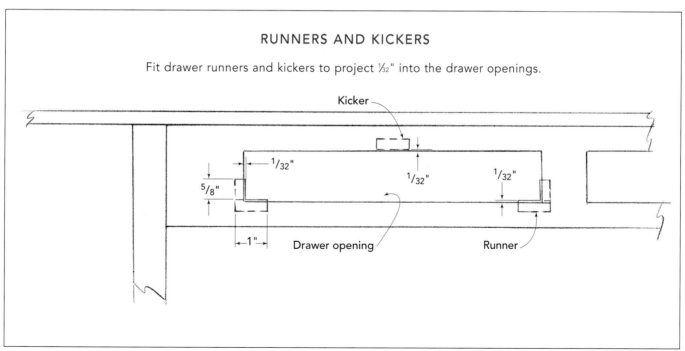

Kicker

1/32"

1/32"

1/32"

5/8"

1"

Drawer opening

Runner

Photo G: Saw the tenon shoulders using the saw's miter gauge and a stop block clamped to the rip fence to register the cut. The stop block prevents kickback that can result from pinching a crosscut piece between the blade and the fence.

the shoulders. Next, use a mortising gauge to lay out the tenon thickness, centering it on the apron (see "Apron Tenon Detail" on p. 50).

5. Saw the tenon shoulders on the table saw (see **photo G**). A stop block clamped to the rip fence in front of the blade registers the workpiece for the shoulder cut. Using the stop block also prevents the kickback that can result from using the fence itself for a stop.

6. Saw the tenon cheeks using a tenoning jig on the table saw (see **photo H**). I always saw the tenons a bit thick and then trim them to size with a rabbet plane during final fitting.

7. Saw the tenon haunches. I mark them out by hand and quickly cut them with a handsaw.

8. Saw or plane the ends of the tenons to 45 degrees so they will meet inside the leg mortises. Then round over the top edge of the tenon to approximate the radius of the mortise.

9. Finish up the aprons by planing them smooth.

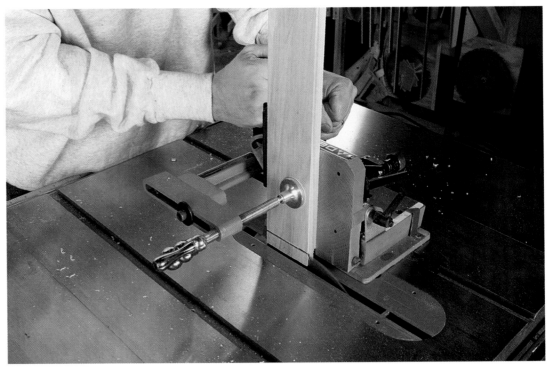

Photo H: Saw the tenon cheeks using a tenoning jig.

Assembling the carcase

1. Dry-fit the carcase to make sure everything fits snugly, but not too tightly. You should be able to push all of the joints together with firm hand pressure. Trim or shim parts as necessary to correct any ill fits.

2. Glue the legs to the side aprons, applying the glue to both the mortises and the tenons. Make sure that the legs are lying flat, with the tapers facing up. To prevent the legs from cocking out of line, make sure your clamping pressure is directly in line with the aprons. Check for square by comparing diagonal measurements. Let the glue dry thoroughly.

3. Glue the side assemblies to the front and back aprons. Check that the diagonals across the top match and make sure the carcase is standing on a level surface while it dries.

4. Make the screw blocks that will fasten the top to the carcase. Drill the screw holes in them, then glue them to the aprons (see **photo I**). After the glue dries, elongate the holes in the front and rear aprons with a rat-tail file to allow for cross-grain movement of the top.

Making and fitting the drawer runners and kickers

1. Thickness plane enough stock to make all of the $\frac{5}{16}$-in.-thick runners and kickers. Rip the pieces to final width and crosscut them to about 10 in. long for now.

2. Mark the final length of each runner and kicker piece while holding it in position in the carcase. Aim for a tight fit. With the two-piece runners, first fit the bottom piece and then the side piece. Draw a witness mark across the two while they're in place. Afterward, glue them together, carefully lining up the witness mark.

3. Glue and toenail the kickers into their notches with a couple of finish nails, front and back.

4. Position the runners in their apron grooves so that the front end of each projects $\frac{1}{32}$ in. into the drawer opening. Plane or shim the

Photo I: Glue the tabletop screw blocks to the aprons. Elongate the holes in the front and rear aprons to accommodate crossgrain movement of the tabletop.

runners if necessary to adjust the projection. Then remove them for now. You'll glue and nail them in place after fitting the drawers.

MAKING AND FITTING THE DRAWERS

Making the parts

The drawers are so tiny that dovetail joints are unnecessary. The rabbeted and nailed joint at the front is plenty strong.

1. Thickness plane stock for the drawers to ⁵⁄₁₆ in., then cut the pieces to size.
2. Saw or rout the dados and grooves as shown in "Drawer Construction."

3. Turn the pulls to the shape shown or buy them to your liking.

Assembling and fitting the drawers

1. Dry-fit the drawers, clamping the joints tightly; then measure for the ¼-in.-thick plywood bottoms. Aim for a tight fit, because each bottom will help square up its drawer.
2. Glue and nail the sides to the front and back, being careful not to spill glue into the bottom grooves. Slide the bottom into place, set the drawer on a known flat surface, and check for square by measuring the diagonals. Let the glue dry thoroughly.
3. Place the drawer runners, unglued, into their grooves. Then check the fit of each

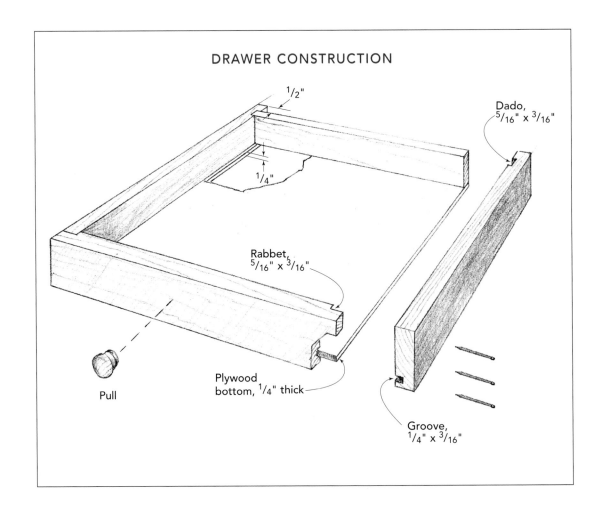

DRAWER CONSTRUCTION

1/2"

Dado, ⁵⁄₁₆" x ³⁄₁₆"

1/4"

Rabbet, ⁵⁄₁₆" x ³⁄₁₆"

Pull

Plywood bottom, ¹⁄₄" thick

Groove, ¹⁄₄" x ³⁄₁₆"

drawer against its opening. It should be very tight at this point.

4. Handplane the top and bottom edges of each drawer until it slides nicely into its opening, leaving about $\frac{1}{32}$ in. clearance all the way around the drawer front. Also plane the drawer front smooth.

5. With the drawer front sitting flush to the face of the apron, adjust the drawer runners until there is about $\frac{1}{32}$ in. clearance on each side of the drawer. Extend reference marks from the runners onto the aprons to register their placement. Glue and toenail the runners into their grooves.

6. Install the drawer stops, which are simply flat-head screws driven into the back apron just behind the ends of the drawer sides (see "Hallway Table" on p. 50).

7. Drill a screw pilot hole into each drawer pull, then attach the pulls with screws driven through the drawer fronts.

FINISHING UP

1. Prepare for finishing by lightly sanding or scraping the exposed surfaces of the carcase and top. Make sure to ease all sharp edges with a plane or sandpaper.

2. Apply your favorite finish to the tabletop and the outside of the carcase. I like to use boiled linseed oil (see "Boiled Linseed Oil Finish" on p. 137).

3. Attach the top to the carcase with screws run through the screw blocks (see **photo J**). Be careful not to drive the screws through the thin top.

Tip: Flat-head screws driven into the rear apron of a carcase make great adjustable drawer stops. Locate them just behind the rear edge of the drawer sides.

Photo J: Screw the top to the carcase through the screw blocks.

SHAKER SEWING TABLE

That which has in itself the highest use possesses the greatest beauty.

—Shaker maxim

I didn't like much of the furniture I grew up with. I remember having an old oak desk that was okay, but the rest of the stuff in our house was awful. It was mostly low-end junk made from poplar and stained to look like cherry. It all had a thick, hard glossy finish, as if it had been dipped in liquid glass.

Years later when I was introduced to Shaker design, I realized that furniture could be beautiful and that its beauty can derive from understatement. Shaker furniture is visually quiet and doesn't rely on fancy moldings, showy veneers, or any virtuosity of craftsmanship. It is designed solely around proportion and utility. You have to study Shaker furniture to appreciate it. Its excellence doesn't scream at you, it doesn't have any "impact": It just is.

This cherry Shaker sewing table was inspired by a design in volume 3 of *Shop Drawings of Shaker Furniture* (Berkshire Traveler Press). It is a very sturdy table with five small drawers, perfect to organize sewing supplies. Although only a few of the table's dimensions were given, I was able to figure out the rest with the help of an architect's rule. No construction details were provided, so I designed a system of joinery that incorporated both traditional joints and biscuit joinery.

Shaker Sewing Table

THIS TABLE IS A TRADITIONAL Shaker design with five drawers. The side and rear aprons join to the legs with haunched tenons. The front rails lock into the legs with half-dovetails. The drawers ride on biscuited web frames, with runners attached as drawer guides. The center web frame also serves as a kicker for the bottom drawers, to keep them from tilting downward when pulled out. The kickers for the top drawers do double-duty as cleats for fastening the top to the carcase.

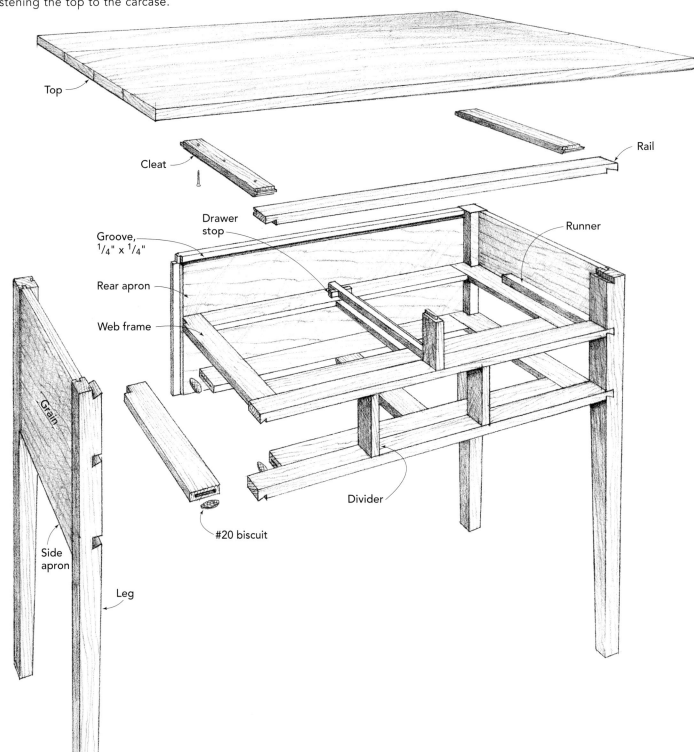

Top

Cleat

Rail

Drawer stop

Runner

Groove, 1/4" x 1/4"

Rear apron

Web frame

Grain

#20 biscuit

Divider

Side apron

Leg

APRON TENON DETAIL

Top View

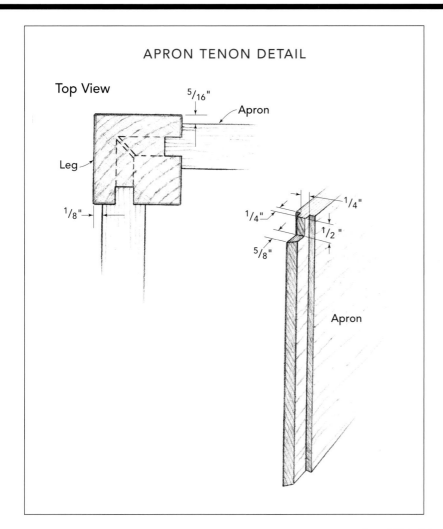

Leg

Apron

5/16"

1/8"

1/4"

1/4"

1/2"

5/8"

Apron

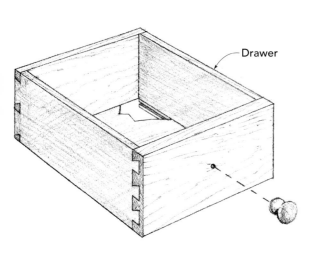

Drawer

DIVIDER TENON DETAIL

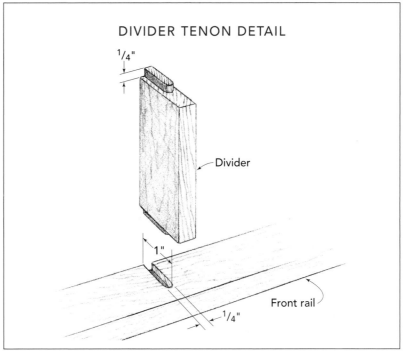

1/4"

Divider

1"

Front rail

1/4"

BUILDING THE TABLE STEP-BY-STEP

CUT LIST FOR SHAKER SEWING TABLE

Top

1	Top	⅝ in. x 18 in. x 30 in.

Carcase

4	Legs	1¼ in. x 1¼ in. x 25⅜ in.
2	Side aprons	⅝ in. x 7⅛ in. x 13⅛ in. (including tenons)
1	Rear apron	⅝ in. x 7⅛ in. x 21 in. (including tenons)
3	Front rails	⅝ in. x 1¼ in. x 20¼ in. (including half-dovetails)
1	Divider	⅝ in. x 1¼ in. x 2⁹⁄₁₆ in. (including tenons)
2	Dividers	⅝ in. x 1¼ in. x 3¹¹⁄₁₆ in. (including tenons)
2	Cleats	¹⁹⁄₃₂ in. x 2 in. x 12⅜ in. (including tenons)
4	Web frame pieces	⅝ in. x 2 in. x 16¼ in.
4	Web frame pieces	⅝ in. x 2 in. x 11⅞ in.
3	Web frame pieces	⅝ in. x 2 in. x 7⅞ in.
4	Side runners	½ in. x ¹¹⁄₁₆ in. x 11⅜ in.
3	Side runners	½ in. x ¹¹⁄₁₆ in. x 11⅞ in.

Drawers

2	Fronts	⅝ in. x 2¹⁄₁₆ in. x 9¼ in.
4	Sides	½ in. x 2¹⁄₁₆ in. x 11¾ in.
2	Backs	½ in. x 1⅝ in. x 9¼ in.
3	Fronts	⅝ in. x 3³⁄₁₆ in. x 5¹⁵⁄₁₆ in.
6	Sides	½ in. x 3³⁄₁₆ in. x 11¾ in.
3	Backs	½ in. x 2¾ in. x 5¹⁵⁄₁₆ in.

THE TABLE CONSISTS OF three basic elements: the top, the carcase, and the drawers. I start with the top, which is dead simple to make. Then I build the carcase, which includes the interior web frames and drawer runners and kickers. Last, I make the drawers to fit their openings in the carcase.

MAKING THE TOP

1. Mill up enough stock to make the 18-in. by 30-in. top. Plane the boards slightly thicker than ⅝ in. You'll want to glue the top up slightly oversize, then rip and crosscut it to final length and width after glue-up.

Photo A: I "spring" the joint by handplaning a slight concavity into the edge of each tabletop board. The resulting ¹⁄₆₄-in. gap at the center ensures that the joint is first and foremost tight at its ends.

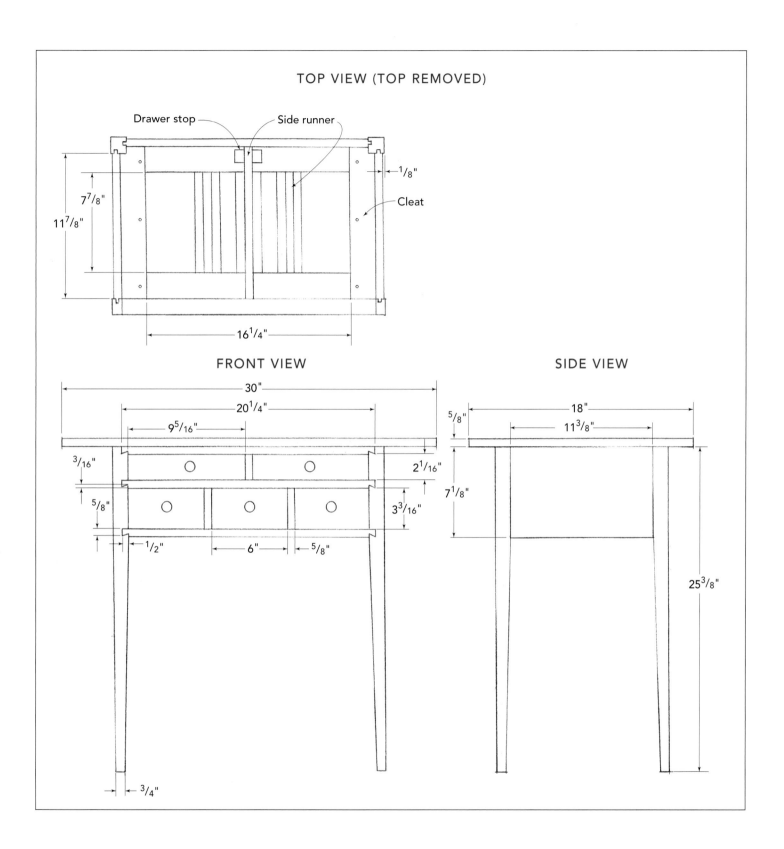

TOP VIEW (TOP REMOVED)

Drawer stop

Side runner

$1/8"$

Cleat

$7^7/8"$

$11^7/8"$

$16^1/4"$

FRONT VIEW

SIDE VIEW

$30"$

$20^1/4"$

$9^5/16"$

$18"$

$5/8"$

$11^3/8"$

$3/16"$

$2^1/16"$

$7^1/8"$

$5/8"$

$3^3/16"$

$1/2"$

$6"$

$5/8"$

$25^3/8"$

$3/4"$

A Panel-Cutting Jig

THIS SHOP-BUILT TABLE SAW SLED allows you to cut panels quickly and accurately.

MAKING THE JIG

1. Cut a piece of ¾" thick hardwood plywood to about 20" x 16".
2. Dimension a 20" long strip of hardwood to fit in your table saw's left-hand miter gauge slot.
3. Place the strip in the miter gauge slot and set your table saw's rip fence to about ⅛" to the right of the blade.
4. Run a bead of glue on the strip, then set the panel on top of it, butting the right-hand edge of the panel against the rip fence.
5. Screw the plywood to the strip.
6. When the glue is dry, place the panel back on the table saw, with the strip running in the miter gauge slot, and trim off the edge of the panel. A short length of dowel installed into the end of the strip makes for easy jig retrieval after a cut.

MAKING THE FENCE

1. Cut a piece of ¾" thick hardwood about 2" wide x 29" long.
2. Screw the right-hand end of the fence to the panel.
3. Carefully square the fence to the right-hand edge of the panel, then screw the left-hand end of the fence to the panel.

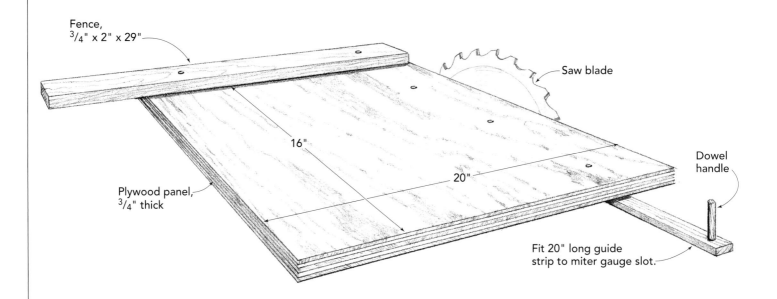

Fence,
³/₄" x 2" x 29"

Saw blade

16"

20"

Dowel handle

Plywood panel,
³/₄" thick

Fit 20" long guide strip to miter gauge slot.

TESTING THE JIG

1. Check for square by making a test cut on a piece of straight-edged material at least 15" wide x 20" long.
2. Crosscut one end using the panel jig, then flip the piece end for end, keeping the same straight edge against the fence, and cut the other end.
3. Measure the diagonals of the test piece. If they don't match to within ¹⁄₆₄", adjust the fence and repeat the test-cut procedure until the diagonals match.

2. Joint the edges of the boards. I "spring" the joint by handplaning a slight concavity in the edges so that about 1/64 in. of light shows between the boards at their centers. That way, I'm sure that the ends of the boards will meet tightly (see **photo A** on p. 68).

3. Edge join the boards. After spreading glue on the edges, I sprinkle a few grains of sand near the ends of the boards to keep them from slipping out of alignment under clamp pressure (see **photo B**).

4. Plane the top to its final thickness of 5/8 in. Rip it to final width, then crosscut it to length using a panel-cutting jig on the table saw (see "A Panel-Cutting Jig").

MAKING THE CARCASE

The carcase is not as complicated as it might seem, although it does have a lot of parts. You'll make the parts for the outside of the carcase first—the legs, aprons, and front rails—and dry-fit them together. Then you'll make the interior web frames, runners, and kickers to fit. Last, you'll glue up the carcase in several stages.

Photo B: A few grains of sand sprinkled into the glue at the ends and center of an edge joint prevent the boards from slipping out of alignment under clamp pressure.

Photo C: I use a commercial tapering jig to saw the taper on the legs.

Photo D: Remove
the saw marks on
the tapers with a
smoothing plane.

Making the legs

1. Mill the 1¼-in.-square by 25⅜-in.-long
blanks for the legs.

2. Using a tapering jig on the table saw, cut
tapers on both inside faces of each leg, as
shown in **photo C** on p. 71. Each taper begins
7½ in. from the top of the leg and diminishes
to ¾ in. at the foot. After sawing, plane the
tapers smooth (see **photo D**).

3. Using a mortising gauge, lay out the mortises for the apron tenons (see **photo E**). The
aprons are inset ⅛ in. from the legs, so set
the mortise back ³⁄₁₆ in. from the outer face of
the leg, as shown in "Apron Tenon Detail"
on p. 67.

4. Rout out the ¹⁵⁄₁₆-in.-deep haunched mortises using a ¼-in.-diameter bit. The mortises in
the rear legs meet inside the leg.

Making the aprons

1. Mill enough ⅝-in.-thick stock to make the
aprons, then cut the pieces to size.

Photo E: Use a
mortising gauge
to lay out the leg
mortises. Remember
that the aprons are
set back ⅛ in. from
the outer faces of
the legs.

2. Cut the tenons to fit the mortises in the legs. I cut them on the table saw using a tenoning jig, sawing them a bit fat and then trimming them with a rabbet plane for a snug fit in their mortises. Cut the haunch by hand and round over the haunch shoulder and bottom edge of the tenon to match the rounded ends of the mortise. Miter the ends of the tenons that meet inside the rear legs.

Making and fitting the rails and dividers

1. Mill enough ⅝-in. by 1¼-in. stock to make the three rails and three dividers, then cut the pieces to length.

2. Lay out the ½-in.-long half-dovetails on the ends of the rails. They taper from ⅜ in. at the ends of the rails to ³⁄₁₆ in. at the shoulder of the half-tail.

3. Cut the half-dovetails with a handsaw. Pare to your cut lines with a chisel, if necessary.

4. Lay out the half-dovetail sockets on the legs by tracing them directly from the half-dovetails. Space the sockets as shown in the drawings on p. 69.

5. Cut out the half-dovetail sockets with a handsaw and chisel. Pare the half-dovetails to fit the sockets, if necessary.

6. Lay out the ¼-in.-wide by 1-in.-long stopped dadoes for the dividers (see "Divider Tenon Detail" on p. 67). The best way to do this is to clamp the rails together and mark the dado spacing on the back sides. Unclamp the pieces and extend the marks onto the edges to be cut.

7. Cut the dadoes for the divider tenons. I cut them out by hand with a gent's saw, chisels, and a router plane. You could rout them instead, but there's not much bearing surface for a router and you'll need to rig up a fence of some sort to guide the router straight.

8. Cut the divider tenons. You could saw them by hand, but it's generally quicker and more accurate to cut them on the table saw using a miter gauge extension and stop block.

9. Saw a ¼-in. by ¼-in. groove in the back side of the top rail and a matching groove in the rear apron as shown in "Shaker Sewing Table" (see p. 66). Space the grooves ¼ in. down from the top edge of the carcase. They will house the tenons on the ends of the cleats.

Making the web frames, kickers, and runners

1. Mill enough ⅝-in.-thick stock to make the two web frames, as shown in "Web Frames" (see p. 74).

2. Assemble the web frames, biscuiting and gluing the frame parts together. Although exact sizes for the frames are given, it's wise to make them just a bit oversize in length and width for now. You can trim them to an exact fit to the carcase's interior later.

3. Cut the two cleats to size. Cut a ¼-in. by ¼-in. tongue on both ends of each cleat so that its top face is flush to the top edge of the carcase, as shown in "Cleat, Web Frame, and Runner Placement" (see p. 75).

4. Mill enough ½-in.-thick material to make the seven runners, but don't cut them to the final widths yet. It's best to do that after the carcase is assembled, to accommodate any small errors.

Assembling the carcase

There are a lot of parts to assemble here. If you can, arrange to have a helper on hand.

1. Dry-fit the rail and divider assembly to the front legs to make sure everything fits well. This is also a good time to rehearse your clamping procedure.

2. Glue and clamp the dividers to the rails, making sure everything is squared up well and that all edges are flush. Let the glue dry thoroughly.

3. Glue and clamp the rear apron between the rear legs. Keep the clamping pressure in line with the apron to prevent cocking the legs out of alignment.

Web Frames

MIDDLE PANEL

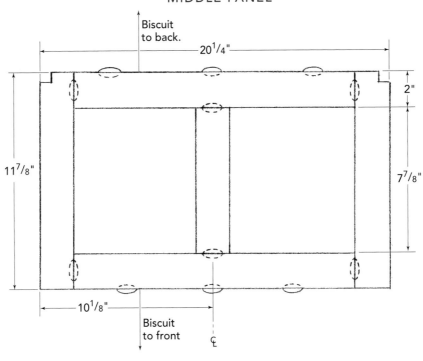

Biscuit to back.

20 1/4"

2"

11 7/8"

7 7/8"

10 1/8"

Biscuit to front

¢

LOWER PANEL

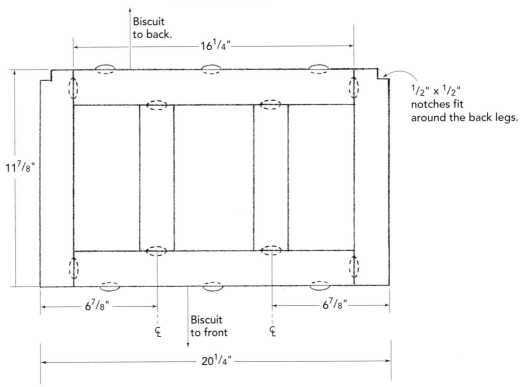

Biscuit to back.

16 1/4"

1/2" x 1/2" notches fit around the back legs.

11 7/8"

6 7/8"

6 7/8"

Biscuit to front

¢

¢

20 1/4"

Cleat, Web Frame, and Runner Placement

To provide proper clearances for the drawers, install the web frames so they project ¹⁄₃₂" into the bottom of the drawer openings. The kickers and web frames should be recessed ¹⁄₃₂" away from the top of the drawer openings. Install the side runners to project ¹⁄₃₂" into the sides of the openings.

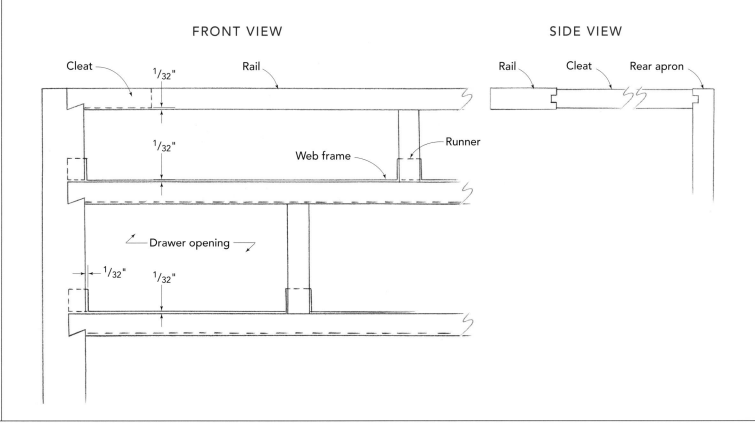

4. After the front rail assembly has dried, glue it between the front legs. Make sure the rails are flush to the legs and that the entire assembly is square after clamping it.

5. Dry-clamp the side aprons between the front and rear assemblies. Measure for the fit of the web frames inside the assembly. Trim the frames to fit and cut the notches out of the rear corners to accommodate the legs.

6. With the frames sitting in place in the carcase, mark for the center locations of the biscuit slots that will attach the frames to the rails and rear apron. Extend each mark from the frame onto its mating location on the rail or apron.

7. Unclamp the carcase and cut the biscuit slots. Carefully space the rows of slots down from the top of the carcase so that each web frame projects upward by ¹⁄₃₂ in. into its drawer opening (see "Cleat, Web Frame, and Runner Placement").

8. Glue and clamp the web frames, cleats, and side aprons between the front and rear assemblies. Here's where you can really use a helper, because there is so much to handle at once. Compare the diagonal measurements taken across the top of the carcase to make sure that it is dead square while clamped up. Also double-check the spacing of the web frames from the top of the carcase.

9. Fit the runners to the web frames, making sure that they project ¹⁄₃₂ in. into the drawer openings, as shown in "Cleat, Web Frame, and Runner Placement" on p. 75. Glue them in place, ensuring that they are square to the face of the carcase.

MAKING THE DRAWERS

The drawers in this sewing table are joined with half-blind dovetails at the front and through dovetails at the rear (see "Drawers"). I used cherry for the sides and backs of my drawers, but you could just as easily use pine or aspen. You'll build the drawers to exactly fit their openings from top to bottom, then plane them after assembly to create a ¹⁄₃₂-in. gap all around the drawer front.

Dimensioning the parts

1. Mill enough stock to ½ in. to make the drawer sides and backs. Then mill enough stock to make the ⅝-in.-thick fronts. Make sure that all of the side pieces and fronts are slightly wider than the height of the drawer openings.

2. To ensure the best possible drawer fit, mark the widths of all of the side and front pieces directly from the height of the drawer openings.

3. Rest a length of drawer side stock for one of the upper drawers on the middle rail, and then mark where the stock meets the top of the drawer opening.

4. Set your table saw fence to this distance and rip the stock for the sides and fronts for both upper drawers to this width. Repeat the procedure for the stock for the lower drawers.

5. Cut the drawer side stock to length.

6. Mark the lengths of the drawer fronts and backs directly from the drawer openings.

7. Cut one end of each piece square and then place it against one side of its drawer opening.

8. Make a mark on the piece at the other end of the drawer opening, subtract ¹⁄₁₆ in., and crosscut the pieces to that length. Note on each drawer front which opening it fits.

9. Next, saw or rout a ¼-in. by ¼-in. groove into the drawer sides and fronts to accept the plywood bottoms. Then rip the drawer backs

Photo F: Use a marking gauge to scribe a line that defines the length of the half-blind dovetails in the drawer fronts.

Drawers

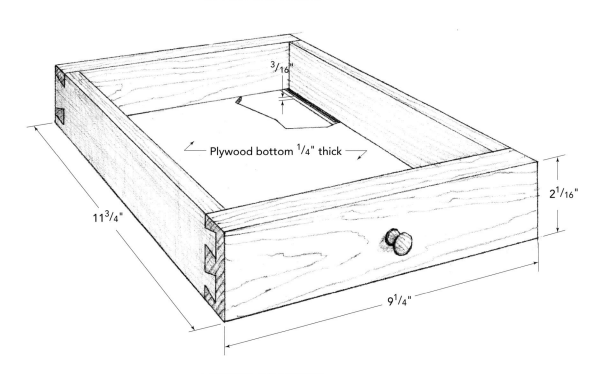

3/16"

Plywood bottom 1/4" thick

2 1/16"

11 3/4"

9 1/4"

LOWER DRAWERS

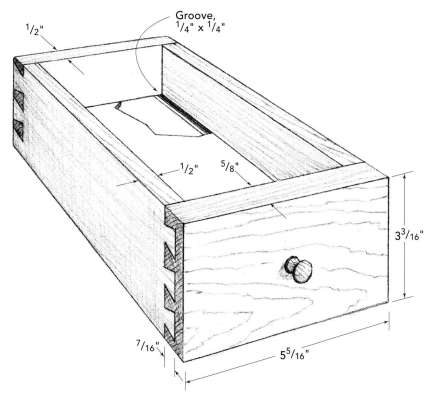

Groove, 1/4" x 1/4"

1/2"

1/2"

5/8"

3 3/16"

7/16"

5 5/16"

THE TRIANGLE MARKING SYSTEM

The triangle marking system is a time-honored approach to marking out pieces for position in preparation for assembly. The principle is simple: A triangle is laid out in segments, as shown here, onto workpieces to be joined together. The triangle quickly identifies the face, side, or edge of the pieces as well as the left and right sides and top and bottom (or front and back). When marking out multiples, such as identical drawers, add a tick mark or number to one side of the triangle segment, as shown here.

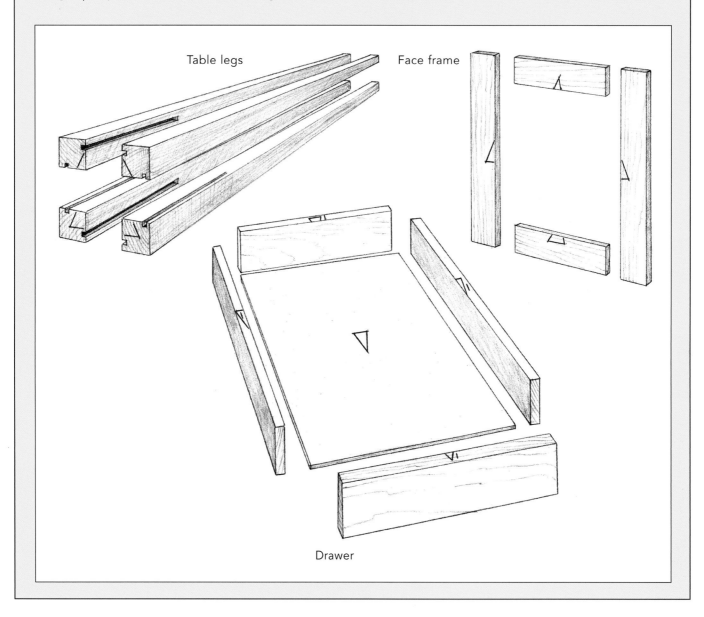

Table legs

Face frame

Drawer

Photo G: Make the initial cuts for the half-blind pins by angling the front-to-rear direction of the saw at 8 to 12 degrees while holding the walls of the saw plumb. Tilt the saw upward to cut between your two marking-gauge lines.

Photo H: Complete the initial pin cuts by inserting an old scraper into the saw kerf and tapping it down to the pin baseline.

to width, which is the distance from the top of a drawer side to the top of the bottom groove (see "Drawers" on p. 77).

Making the dovetail joints

1. Mark the drawer parts for position to keep them straight when you cut the joinery (see "The Triangle Marking System").

2. Lay out and cut the through dovetails for the drawers' rear joints (see "Cutting the Dovetail Joints" on p. 42). The upper drawers get a single dovetail per side. The lower drawers get two per side.

3. Set a marking gauge to ½ in. and mark a line to establish the thickness of the pins on the end of each drawer front (see **photo F** on p. 76).

4. Mark the baseline for the pins on the inside of the drawer fronts ½ in. from the ends.

5. Saw the pins. The upper drawers get one full pin and two half-pins. The lower drawers get two full pins and two half-pins. As with through dovetails, there is no need to lay out the pins. Clamp the drawer front in the bench vise with the inside of the drawer facing you, then saw on a diagonal to the gauge line using a backsaw with very little set (see **photo G**).

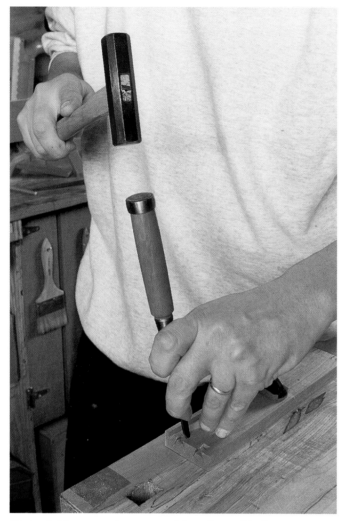

Photo I: Chop out the waste with a sharp chisel.

Photo J: Use a long, thin awl to trace the outline of the pins onto the drawer sides to mark out the half-blind dovetails.

6. Place an old scraper into the saw kerf and tap down to the gauge line to complete the cut (see **photo H** on p. 79). Go easy here. If you tap too hard, you can split the wood.

7. Chisel out the pin waste, as shown in **photo I**.

8. Mark for the tails. Stand the drawer front on end on each drawer side and trace the shapes of the pins using an awl with a long, slim point (see **photo J**).

9. Saw and chop out the tails to fit.

Assembling the drawers

1. Dry-assemble the drawers to make sure the joints fit well (see **photo K**). While the drawers are assembled, measure for the bottoms and cut them all.

2. Glue up the drawers. For each drawer, brush glue on all mating pin and tail surfaces, then tap each side onto the front and back. Before the glue sets up, slide the bottom into its grooves, square the drawer up, and then nail the bottom onto the drawer back from underneath.

Photo K: Test the fit of the joint by lightly tapping the tails into the sockets.

3. Turn the pulls (see "Sewing Table Pull"). It's nice to make them from a contrasting wood. I used black walnut.

Fitting the drawers to their openings

1. Set each drawer on the bench to make sure it sits flat. If it rocks a bit from corner to corner, plane the high corners until it sits flat. Then plane the top and bottom edges smooth.
2. Test-fit each drawer into its opening to make sure that it slides in and out easily. If necessary, plane a bit more off the top and bottom to achieve a consistent ¹⁄₃₂-in. gap around the drawer front.

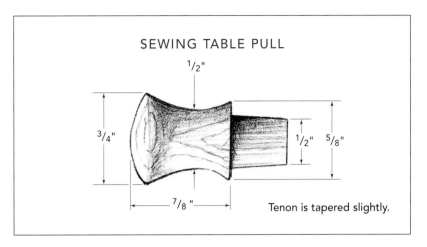

SEWING TABLE PULL

¹⁄₂"

³⁄₄"

¹⁄₂" ⁵⁄₈"

⁷⁄₈"

Tenon is tapered slightly.

3. Align the drawer front flush to the outside face of the carcase rails and mark the runners for the drawer stop placement. Make the drawer stops and glue them to the runners.

FINISHING UP

1. Sand all exposed surfaces lightly as needed to prepare for finishing.
2. Attach the top by screwing it on through the cleats.
3. Apply your favorite finish. I put on three coats of boiled linseed oil (see "Boiled Linseed Oil Finish" on p. 137).
4. Attach the pulls by gluing them into holes drilled in the drawer fronts.

OVAL COFFEE TABLE

When a customer requested a living room coffee table for her small apartment, we decided that an oval table would fit the bill. An oval coffee table can save a bit of space, while still offering plenty room for large books.

The problem with an oval top is that it can look awkward sitting on a rectangular base with straight aprons. Rather than bend aprons to suit the oval, I came up with the X-shaped base you see here, which proved to be a simple, elegant solution. It's easy to make, and the sawed curves of the legs and rails play nicely against the oval top. I also planed a wide bevel on the underside edges of the top to create the appearance of lightness.

Although this walnut table is one of the simplest projects in the book, many people find it rather fancy. In a room full of intricately styled furniture, it can serve as a prim yet unpretentious accent to a sofa or set of easy chairs. On the other hand, it can also look comfortably informal in a den or bedroom.

Oval Coffee Table

THIS LOVELY LITTLE WALNUT TABLE is one of the easiest projects in this book. The oval top sits on the X-shaped base, which is made up of two leg-and-rail assemblies that cross each other at the center. Because the loose-fitting lap joint at the center is not glued, the two leg-and-rail assemblies can move independently of each other to accommodate seasonal movement of the top.

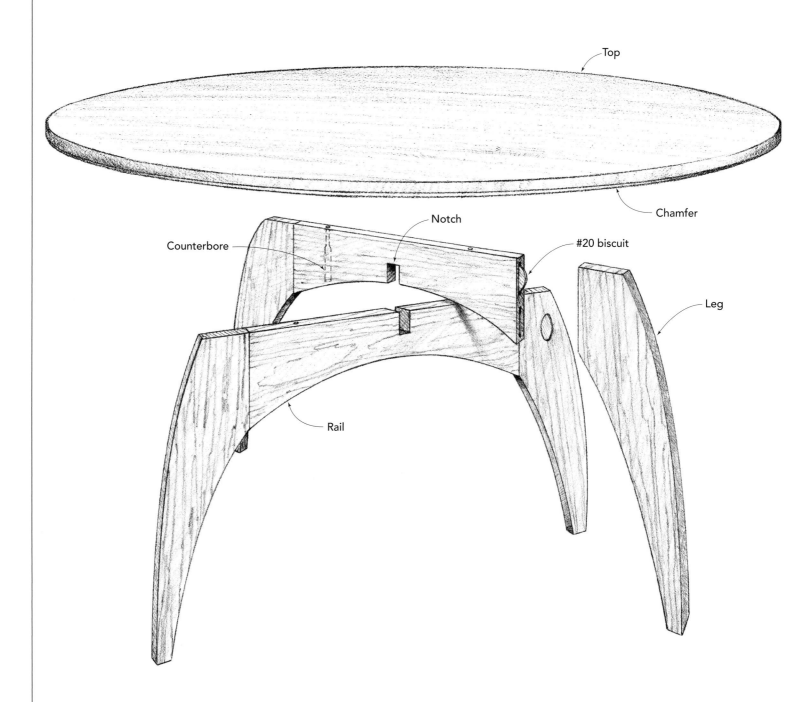

BASE ANGLE DETAIL

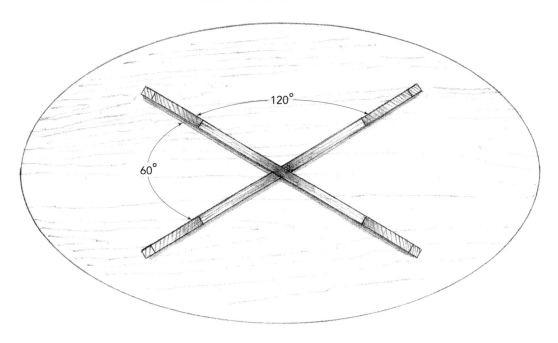

120°

60°

CHAMFER DETAIL

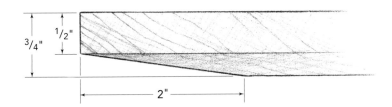

3/4"

1/2"

2"

CUT LIST FOR OVAL COFFEE TABLE

Top		
1	Oval blank	¾ in. x 24 in. x 44 in.
Base		
2	Rail blanks	¾ in. x 4⅞ in. x 18 in.
4	Legs	¾ in. x 6½ in. x 16¾ in.

BUILDING THE TABLE STEP-BY-STEP

THE TABLE IS COMPOSED of three basic components: the top and the two identical leg-and-rail assemblies that make up the base. The top is made of boards glued up to width, then marked and sawed to the oval shape. The legs are marked and cut to rough shape using plywood templates, then joined to the rails and cut to their final shape. Biscuits make for easy leg-to-rail joinery.

MAKING THE TOP

Making the blank
1. Mill up enough ¹³⁄₁₆-in.-thick stock to make a 24-in. by 44-in. blank.
2. Edge glue the boards to make the blank.

Photo A: Carefully cut the oval out of the blank with a jigsaw. The more smoothly you cut the curves, the less cleanup work you'll have to do.

3. Handplane or belt sand the blank to a smooth ¾-in. thickness.

Laying out the ellipse
The symmetrical oval of this tabletop is properly called an ellipse, because an oval can also be egg shaped. There are a number of ways and jigs to lay out an ellipse. I use a framing square and a layout stick.

1. Make a layout stick from ¾-in.-square stock and drill a hole for a pencil in one end. Use a yellow- or white-colored pencil, because lighter lines show up better on the dark walnut wood.
2. Mark two points on the layout stick, measuring out from the center of the pencil hole. The distance to the first mark should be 11 in., which is one-half the length of the minor ellipse axis. The second mark should be 21 in. away, which is one-half the length of the major axis.
3. Drive a brad through each of these points so that the head of the brad projects about ¹⁄₁₆ in. Clip off the other end of each brad.
4. Scribe the ellipse on the top blank by follow the steps in "Laying Out an Ellipse."

Cutting and chamfering the top
1. Cut the oval from the blank with a jigsaw or scroll bowsaw. It's difficult to maneuver a piece this large on a bandsaw; follow the line carefully (see **photo A**).
2. Clamp the piece in the bench and clean up the edges with a spokeshave or file (see **photo B** on p. 88).
3. Mark for the chamfer on the underside of the top, as shown in "Chamfer Detail" on p. 85. With the top upside down on the bench, use a marking gauge to scribe a line 2 in. from the edge all the way around (see photo C on p. 88).

Laying Out an Ellipse

LAY OUT AN ELLIPSE one quadrant at a time, following these steps.

1. Mark the centerlines on the workpiece, then align and clamp a framing square to the lines.
2. Place the layout stick's outermost brad against the corner of the square, with the other brad against the leg of the square.

3. Holding the brads against the square, slide the layout stick as shown, which moves the pencil along one quadrant of the ellipse.
4. Repeat the setup for the remaining quadrants.

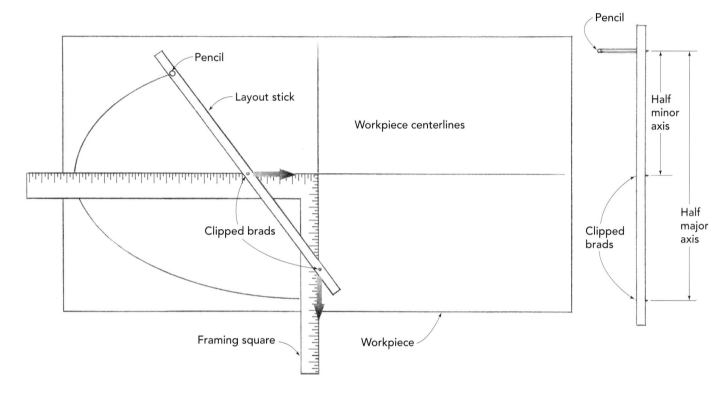

SIDE VIEW OF LAYOUT STICK

Pencil

Layout stick

Pencil

Workpiece centerlines

Half minor axis

Half major axis

Clipped brads

Clipped brads

Framing square

Workpiece

To lay out the oval top, I guide the two brads in the layout stick against the edges of a square clamped to the workpiece. A white pencil shows up clearly on walnut.

Photo B: Clean up the sawn edges of the top using a spokeshave and file.

Photo C: Use a marking gauge to define the inside edge of the chamfer on the underside of the tabletop.

Photo D: Registering a marking gauge against the top face of the tabletop, mark a line on the edge of the top to define the outer edge of the chamfer.

Photo E: Plane a gently sloping chamfer on the underside of the tabletop, staying between your gauge lines.

4. Mark a line completely around the edge ½ in. down from the top (see **photo D**).

5. Plane away the material within the gauge lines to form a long, gentle chamfer around the bottom edge (see **photo E**). When viewing the table from above, the top will appear to be ½ in. thick.

6. Smooth the chamfer with a sanding block and slightly round over the sharp edges on the top.

MAKING THE BASE

Making the legs and rails

To make the base, you'll cut the legs to rough shape, then join them to the rail blanks. After biscuit joining a pair of legs to each rail, you'll cut the interior curves of the assemblies to final shape. Last, you'll notch the leg-and-rail assemblies to fit together into an X-shape.

1. Using ¼-in.-thick plywood, make a template for the legs and a half template for the rails (see "Leg Pattern" and "Rail Half-Pattern"). When making the leg template, make sure that the foot is parallel to the top of the leg.

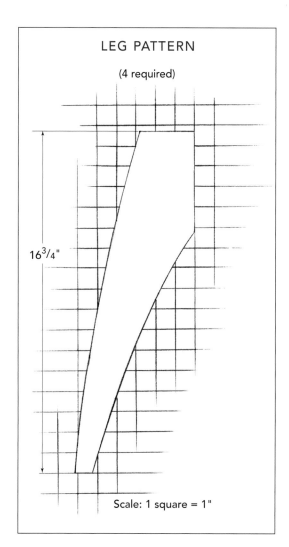

LEG PATTERN

(4 required)

$16^{3}/_{4}$"

Scale: 1 square = 1"

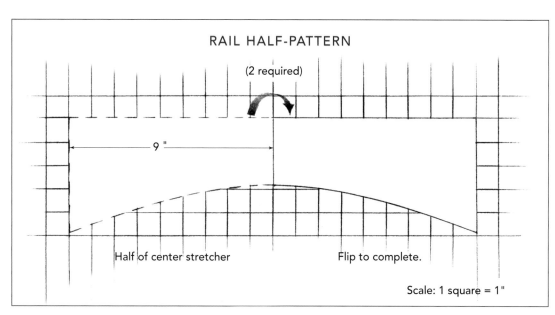

RAIL HALF-PATTERN

(2 required)

9"

Half of center stretcher   Flip to complete.

Scale: 1 square = 1"

2. Thickness stock for the legs and rails to ¾ in. For the legs, use boards at least 6½ in. wide. Joint one edge of the stock afterward. The jointed edge will become the shoulder of the leg that meets the rail.

3. Lay out the legs using your template. To make best use of your stock, you can lay out the legs in stepped fashion on a single longer board, as shown in "Leg Layout," instead of the four boards listed in the Cut List.

4. Cut out the legs. See "Leg Cutting Sequence" for a safe, accurate approach to sawing out legs that are laid out in stepped fashion. Note that the inside edge of each leg is cut oversize for right now. After assembly, you'll trim it and the rail curve to final shape.

Making the leg-and-rail assemblies

1. Cut the rectangular rail blanks to size.

2. Using the rail half-pattern, trace the curve onto the rail blanks one half at a time.

3. Mark out biscuit slots to join the legs and rails. Measuring down from the top edge of a rail, make two marks, one at 1¼ in. and one at 3⅝ in. Extend these marks onto the other rails and onto each leg.

4. Cut a slot for a #20 biscuit at each location (see **photo F** on p. 92).

5. Apply glue to the slots, the biscuits, and the joint faces. Double-coating the end grain on the rails will prevent a starved glue joint.

6. Clamp the joint with a deep-throat bar clamp. A handscrew keeps the bar clamp from sliding off of the curved edges of the legs (see **photo G** on p. 92). Alternatively, you could use hot-melt glue to attach the offcuts from the curve onto the leg to provide parallel surfaces for clamping.

7. When the glue is dry, unclamp the assembly and cut the curves on the rails and insides of the legs. Make sure that the curves meet nicely at their juncture. (Save the waste from the rail curve. You may want to use it as a platform for drilling the screw holes in the rails, as explained later.)

8. Smooth the curves, if necessary, with a spokeshave or patternmaker's rasp. You can easily shave off rasp marks with a hand scraper. I follow up by sanding with 80-grit

LEG LAYOUT

To maximize stock, lay out the legs in a stepped fashion, carefully aligning the joint face to the jointed edge of the board.

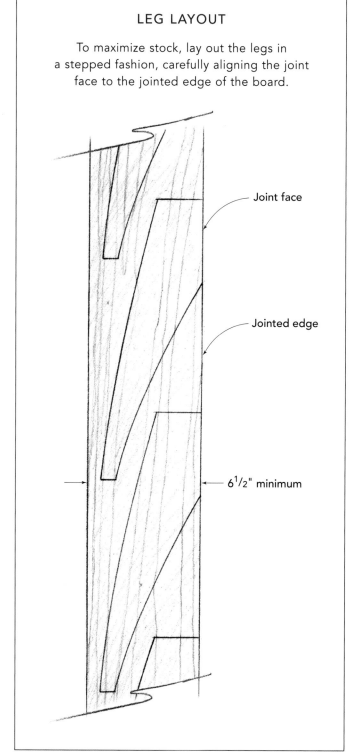

Joint face

Jointed edge

6$^1/_2$" minimum

LEG CUTTING SEQUENCE

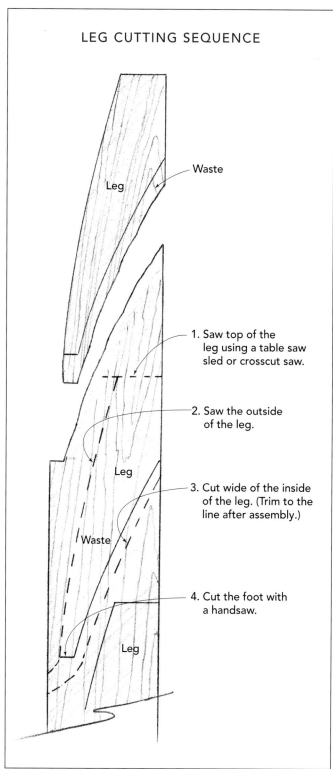

Waste

Leg

1. Saw top of the leg using a table saw sled or crosscut saw.

2. Saw the outside of the leg.

Leg

3. Cut wide of the inside of the leg. (Trim to the line after assembly.)

Waste

4. Cut the foot with a handsaw.

Leg

Photo F: Cut two slots for #20 biscuits into the joint face of each leg and into the ends of each rail.

Photo G: I clamp two legs to each rail using a deep-throat bar clamp. A handscrew clamped to the rail prevents the bar clamp from sliding off the curves of the legs.

Photo H: Plane or sand the leg-to-rail joint faces smooth.

paper on an orbital sander, smoothing the edges to a uniform curve.

9. Plane or sand the joints smooth as shown (see **photo H**).

10. Rout a ¼-in. roundover on all except the top edges of the assemblies and then sand the roundovers smooth.

Joining the base assemblies

The leg-and-rail assemblies cross each other at 60 degrees and are joined with a half-lap notch.

1. Mark the end-to-end centerpoint on the face of one rail, then extend the line down to and across the bottom edge of the rail at 90 degrees.

2. Set a bevel gauge to 60 degrees and mark a line through the center of the 90 degree line that you made on the rail's bottom edge.

3. With the bevel gauge still set to 60 degrees, mark two lines ¹³⁄₁₆ in. apart, centered on the previous line (see **photo I** on p. 94). These lines determine the notch shoulders.

4. With a combination square, extend the notch shoulder lines across the faces of the rails. Mark the bottom of the notch halfway down from the top of the rail.

5. Saw to the shoulder lines with a handsaw (see **photo J** on p. 94). Chisel out the waste to the bottom of the notch.

6. Center the second leg-and-rail assembly in the notch you just cut and trace the shoulders from the first notch onto the second rail.

7. Separate the assemblies and extend the lines you just drew completely across the face of the rail. Then use a combination square to gauge the distance between the top of the first notch and the top of its rail. Place the square against the top edge of the second rail and

Photo I: To establish the shoulders of the notch in the rails, lay out parallel lines at 60 degrees to the edge and centered on the rail.

Photo J: To cut the notch, first saw the shoulders, then chisel out the waste to the finished depth of the notch.

transfer the distance to locate the bottom of the second notch.

8. Saw out and chisel the second notch in the same manner as the first. When the two notches are lapped, the tops of the rails should be flush.

ATTACHING THE TOP

The top is screwed to the base through the rails. Because the rails are fairly deep, you'll need to counterbore them for the screws.

1. Measure in 6¼ in. from the top corners of each leg-and-rail assembly and mark a line squarely across the top edge of the rail. Then extend each line squarely down and across the bottom of each rail.

2. Chuck a ⅝-in.-diameter bit into your drill press for drilling the counterbores into the bottom edges of the rails. The idea here is to allow a 2½-in.-long screw to project about ½ in. from the top of the rail. You sure don't want the screw to go through the tabletop. To be safe, gauge a line on the face of the rail about 2 in. from the top (straight) edge, and use the gauge line to set your drill press stop. It's also a good idea to clamp the rail to the drill press table for drilling these large holes into a curved edge.

3. Finish up the holes by drilling the rest of the way through the rail with a ³⁄₁₆-in.-diameter bit. Most ³⁄₁₆-in. drill bits are too short to reach through from the bottom of the rail, so you'll need to drill these holes in from the top edge. You can do this by hand, using the layout lines on the faces of the rails to help guide you. Or you can temporarily attach the waste from the rail curve cutout to create a drill press platform.

4. To attach the top, place it upside down on the workbench, with the base centered on it. Drive a 2½-in.-long coarse-thread, self-tapping drywall screw through each rail into the top (see **photo K**).

5. Stand the table on a known flat surface to check for wobble. If necessary, scribe the feet to the flat surface and trim them with a hand-saw to level the table.

Photo K: To attach the top, drive two 2½-in.-long self-tapping dry-wall screws through the counterbored holes in the rail and into the tabletop.

FINISHING UP

I finished the table with boiled linseed oil, which deepens the walnut to a rich brown color (see "Boiled Linseed Oil Finish" on p. 137). For a glossier finish, wax can be applied after oiling, but be sure to use dark wax or the finish will "haze," showing white in the pores of the wood.

Glass-Top Display Table

John McDonald, a California furniture maker, designed and built this table to display and protect small, fragile art objects. Its glass top showcases the items within.

This piece embodies a number of elegant, thoughtful touches. At first viewing, you notice the lovely wood-framed glass top and the subtle ¼-in. taper on the insides of the legs. Any more of a taper, and the table would look barrel-chested and top heavy. Any less, and the legs would seem boxy.

On closer investigation, you notice that the plate glass, with its slightly rounded top edges, sits 1⁄16 in. proud of the tabletop—a nice touch.

Some display tables require removal of the glass top to access the inside, but McDonald's table employs a drawer whose front is cleverly disguised to look like one of the table's aprons. Because a drawer pull would spoil the illusion, the drawer front projects ⅛ in. below the table's front rail for finger access.

A defining characteristic of this table is the drawer bottom, which doubles as a background for the displayed items. Rather than using a single piece of hardwood or plywood for the drawer bottom, McDonald made it using frame-and-panel construction.

McDonald used straight-grained, rift-sawn, red birch for his table, but I used silver maple. Almost any wood, except exotic, showy ones, would be appropriate for this quiet piece.

Glass-Top Display Table

THIS TABLE IS DESIGNED to showcase art objects placed inside. A glass top resting in a rabbet cut into the top frame serves as the tabletop and display window. Art objects are held in a drawer whose front is disguised to look like one of the table's aprons. The frame-and-panel drawer bottom provides a distinctive background for the display objects.

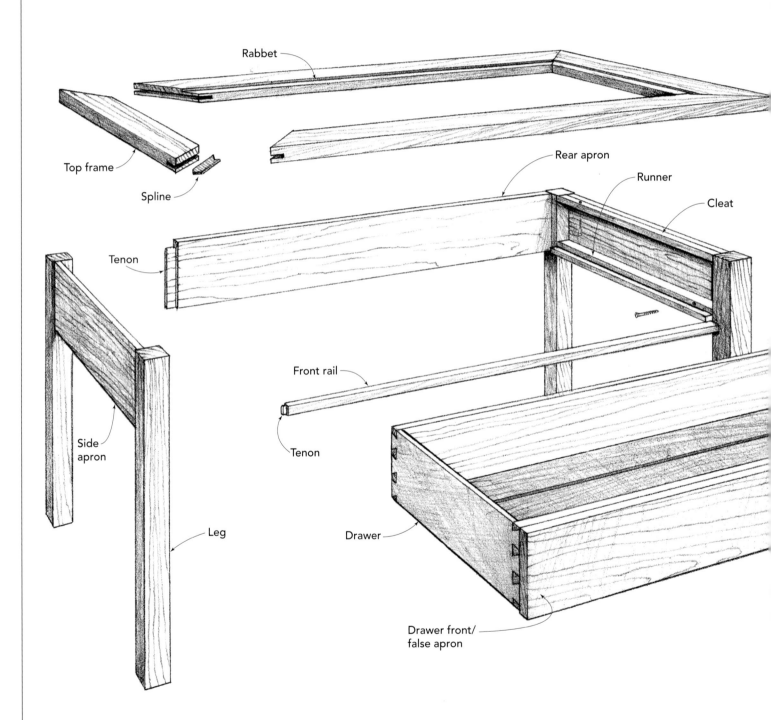

APRON TENON DETAIL

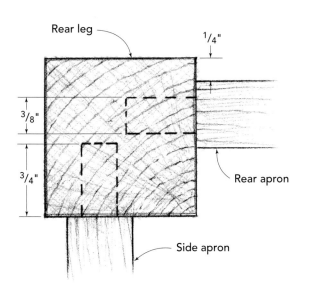

Rear leg

1/4"

3/8"

3/4"

Rear apron

Side apron

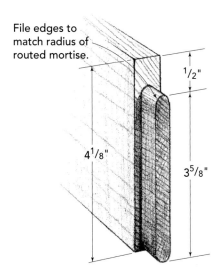

File edges to match radius of routed mortise.

1/2"

4 1/8"

3 5/8"

RAIL TENON DETAIL

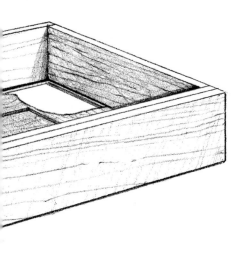

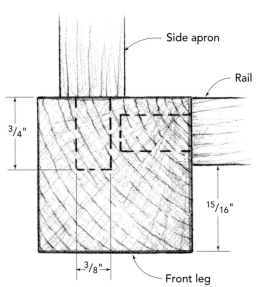

Side apron

Rail

3/4"

3/8"

15/16"

Front leg

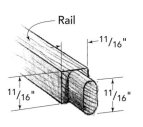

Rail

11/16"

11/16"

11/16"

CUT LIST FOR GLASS-TOP DISPLAY TABLE

Top

2	Frame members	11⁄16 in. x 31⁄8 in. x 211⁄4 in.
2	Frame members	11⁄16 in. x 31⁄8 in. x 331⁄4 in.

Base

4	Legs	15⁄8 in. x 15⁄8 in. x 165⁄16 in.
1	Front rail	11⁄16 in. x 11⁄16 in. x 30 in. (including tenons)
1	Drawer front/false apron	11⁄16 in. x 41⁄8 in. x 281⁄2 in. (including tenons)
1	Rear apron	11⁄16 in. x 41⁄8 in. x 30 in. (including tenons)
2	Side aprons	11⁄16 in. x 41⁄8 in. x 18 in. (including tenons)
2	Drawer runners	1 in. x 1 in. x 161⁄2 in. (with 11⁄16-in. x 11⁄16-in. rabbet)
2	Cleats	11⁄16 in. x 11⁄16 in. x 161⁄2 in.

Drawer

1	Front	1⁄2 in. x 35⁄16 in. x 281⁄2 in.
1	Back	1⁄2 in. x 35⁄16 in. x 281⁄2 in.
2	Sides	1⁄2 in. x 35⁄16 in. x 173⁄4 in.
2	Bottom frame members	1⁄2 in. x 33⁄8 in. x 28 in.
2	Bottom frame members	1⁄2 in. x 33⁄8 in. x 101⁄2 in.
1	Bottom frame member	1⁄2 in. x 31⁄8 in. x 221⁄4 in. (including tenons)
2	Bottom panels	5⁄16 in. x 411⁄16 in. x 221⁄4 in.

THE TABLE CONSISTS OF three elements: the top, the base, and the drawer. I make the top first. That way I can take it to the glass shop to get the glass cut for it while I build the rest of the table. The base is built next. Then I make the drawer to fit its opening.

MAKING THE TOP

The top is simply a mitered frame joined at the corners with splines. For a strong joint, the grain of the spline needs to run perpendicular to the joint line. The inside top edge is rabbeted to accept a piece of 1⁄4-in.-thick tempered glass.

Making the frame

1. Dimension the stock for the frame members. Leave 1 in. or more excess in length.

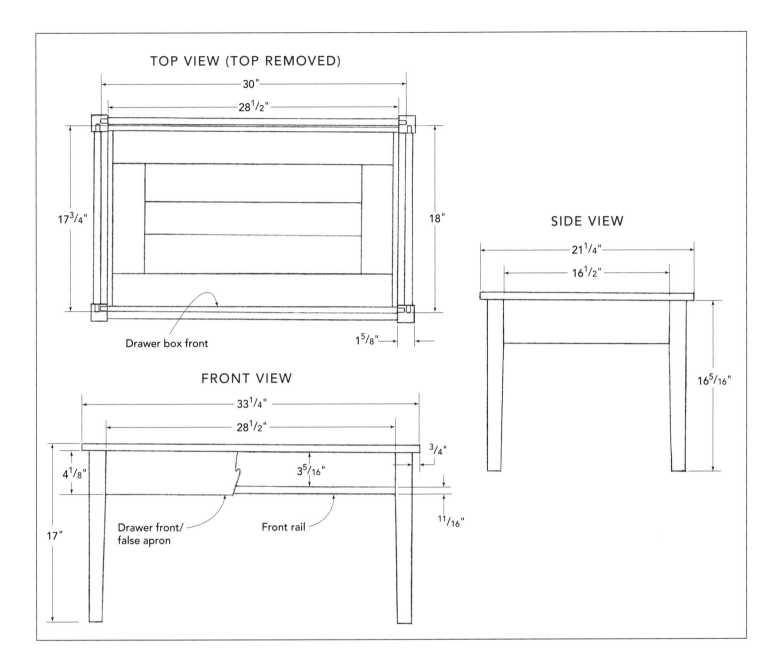

TOP VIEW (TOP REMOVED)

30"

28¹/₂"

17³/₄"

18"

Drawer box front

1⁵/₈"

SIDE VIEW

21¹/₄"

16¹/₂"

16⁵/₁₆"

FRONT VIEW

33¹/₄"

28¹/₂"

3/₄"

4¹/₈"

3⁵/₁₆"

11/₁₆"

17"

Drawer front/
false apron

Front rail

2. Cut the miters on the ends of the frame members. I use a shopmade table saw sled for this (see "A Table Saw Miter Sled" on p. 116). Take care to cut the angles accurately so that the frame lays out square afterward.

3. Cut the ¼-in. by ⅜-in. spline slots in the mitered ends, spacing each one as shown in "Top Frame Corner Detail" on p. 102. I use a dado cutter in the table saw, clamping the workpiece to my tenoning jig.

4. Make the spline stock by ripping a short length of material to 5⅛ in. wide and then

planing it to thickness. Aim for a thickness that fits snugly in the slots. You should be able to insert the spline material with finger pressure only.

5. Crosscut the spline stock into ¾-in. lengths to make the individual splines.

6. Dry-clamp the frame with the splines inserted to make sure everything fits well and to rehearse your clamping procedure.

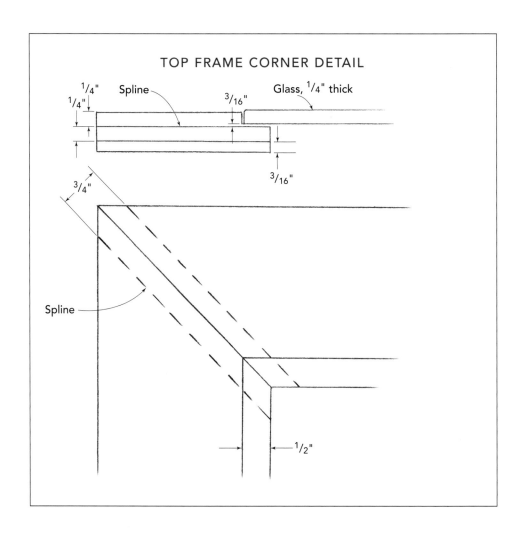

TOP FRAME CORNER DETAIL

1/4"
Spline
3/16"
Glass, 1/4" thick

1/4"

3/16"

3/4"

Spline

1/2"

Photo A: Rout the rabbet for the glass top, moving the router clockwise inside the frame.

Photo C: Clean up the bottom of the rabbet corner with a chisel.

Photo B: The first step in squaring up the corners of the rabbet is to cut the wall using a wide chisel.

I use bar clamps—two over and two under—carefully lining up the corners of the rabbets. You could use a band clamp instead, which will line up the outside corners automatically, then apply extra force with bar clamps where needed to tighten the joint or to better line up the corners.

7. Glue up the frame, working quickly. Make sure the assembly is square and that the corners line up well. Let the assembly dry thoroughly.

8. Trim the projecting excess of the splines with a small handsaw. Then pare the remainder flush to the edges of the frame with a chisel. When paring the outside corner, make sure to cut with the grain, working from the corner inward to prevent tearout.

9. Rout the ½-in.-wide by ³⁄₁₆-in.-deep rabbet for the glass (see **photo A**).

10. Square off the rounded corners left by the router with a wide chisel to cut the rabbet walls (see **photo B**). Work carefully to create a crisp 90 degree corner.

11. Chisel out the waste to the bottom of the rabbet (see **photo C**).

12. Take the completed frame to your local glass shop and have them cut a piece of ¼-in.-thick tempered glass to fit snugly within the rabbets. Ask them to "ease" the upper edges of the glass, rounding them over slightly.

MAKING THE BASE

The base is a simple construct: tenons on the side aprons and the rear apron slip into mortises on the legs. A narrow rail ties the two front legs together and serves as a stop for the drawer front. Two L-shaped drawer runners and two cleats attach to the side aprons.

Making the legs

The legs are made from 1⅝-in.-square stock. Each leg tapers to 1⅜ in. at the foot and is mortised to accept tenons on the ends of the aprons.

1. Saw the stock for the legs to size. McDonald suggests using riftsawn lumber, which displays a straight, sedate figure on all faces, as shown in "Riftsawn Legs."

2. Lay out the tapers on the two inside faces of each leg (see **photo D**). The tapers begin 4⅛ in. from the top of the leg and diminish to 1⅜ in. at the foot.

3. Cut the tapers. You can do this with a tapering jig on the table saw, but because the tapers are so slight, I used a smoothing plane.

4. Lay out the ⅜-in.-wide by 3⅜-in.-long mortises to accept the apron tenons. Don't forget

to include the ¼-in. setback of the apron from the outside face of the leg (see "Apron Tenon Detail" on p. 99).

5. Lay out the ⅜-in.-wide by ¹¹⁄₁₆-in.-long mortise for the front rail (see "Rail Tenon Detail" on p. 99). The mortise begins 3⁵⁄₁₆ in. down from the top of the leg. The ¹⁵⁄₁₆-in. setback from the face of the leg will create a ¼-in. setback for the drawer front/false apron when the drawer is closed.

Photo D: The tapers on the inside faces of the legs begin 4⅛ in. down from the top and diminish to 1⅜ in. at the foot.

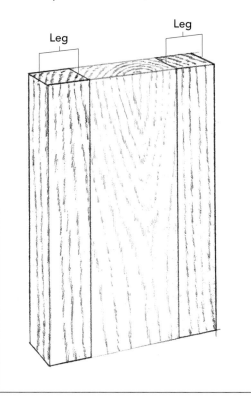

RIFTSAWN LEGS

Table legs cut from riftsawn stock (identified by its diagonal end grain) will display balanced, straight grain on all faces of the legs. Riftsawn stock is often obtained from the edges of a wide plainsawn board, as shown here.

Leg   Leg

6. Rout the ¾-in.-deep apron and rail mortises using a ⅜-in.-diameter straight bit. Use a router fence to guide the cut.

Making the aprons and front rail

1. Plane, rip, and crosscut the aprons and rail to size.

2. Lay out and cut the tenons on the ends of the rear and side aprons. I rip the tenons a bit fat on the table saw using a tenoning jig, then cut the haunch with a handsaw and trim the tenons to a snug fit with a rabbet plane.

3. Round over the edges of the tenons with a file to match the round ends of the routed mortises.

4. Lay out and cut the tenons on the ends of the rail.

Assembling the base and fitting the cleats and runners

1. Dry-clamp the base to make sure that all of the joints fit well and to rehearse your clamping procedures.

2. Glue the legs to the side aprons. Keep the clamp screws in line with the aprons to prevent cocking the legs out of line.

3. Glue the rear apron and front rail between the two side assemblies. Don't overtighten the clamp on the rail. You don't want to bend it. Check the diagonal measurements across the top of the table to make sure that it is square while the glue sets up. Otherwise the drawer won't fit well.

4. Make the cleats and drawer runners, fitting them between the front and rear legs. The runners are made by cutting an ¹¹⁄₁₆-in. by ¹¹⁄₁₆-in. rabbet into 1-in.-square stock.

5. Glue the cleats to the side aprons, aligning them flush to the top of the aprons.

6. Attach the drawer runners. For now, use only one screw at the front end of each. You'll make final adjustments and attachments after fitting the drawer.

MAKING THE DRAWER

The drawer consists of a frame-and-panel bottom that sits in grooves cut into the drawer front, back, and sides. Unlike many drawer bottoms that slide into their grooves from the rear of the assembled drawer, this bottom is totally enclosed within the walls of the box. To ensure a good fit, make the drawer sides first, then make the bottom to fit into its grooves.

Making the drawer sides

1. Dimension the stock for the drawer box front, back, and sides.

2. Cut a ¼-in. by ¼-in. groove in all four pieces for the drawer bottom. Cut the groove ⁵⁄₁₆ in. up from the bottom of the pieces, as shown in "Section through Drawer." This raises the drawer bottom so it doesn't scrape on the front rail.

Tip: To easily clean up white or yellow glue squeeze-out, wait an hour or so until the glue has turned rubbery, then pare or slice it off using a sharp chisel.

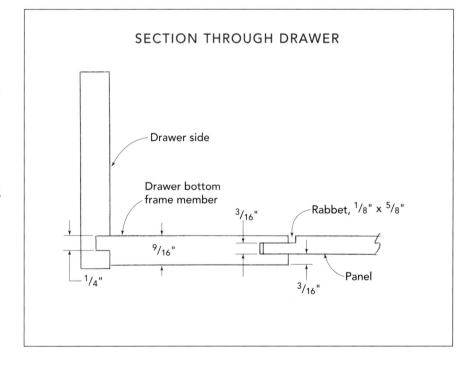

SECTION THROUGH DRAWER

Drawer side

Drawer bottom frame member

Rabbet, ¹⁄₈" x ⁵⁄₈"

Panel

³⁄₁₆"

9⁄16"

³⁄₁₆"

¼"

DRAWER BOTTOM JOINERY

Identical front and back frame members join to the side frame members with glue and biscuits.
The two rabbeted floating panels ride unglued in grooves cut into the frame members.

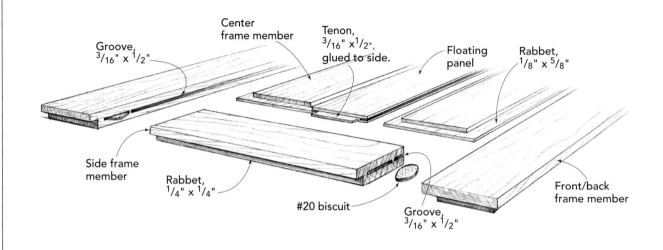

DRAWER BOTTOM ELEVATION (TOP VIEW)

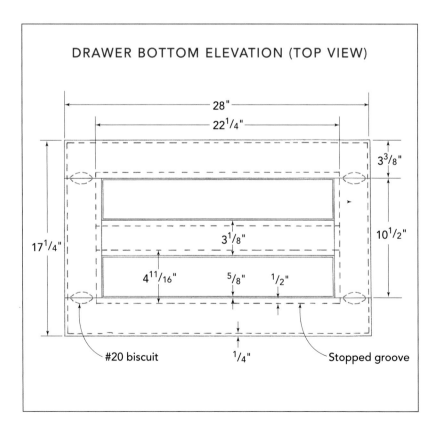

3. Cut the through dovetails for the corner joints of the drawer. Each corner gets three tails and four pins. Make sure the bottom groove runs through the tails, not the pins (see "Cutting the Dovetail Joints" on p. 42 for detailed information).

4. Dry-fit the joints. With the tails tapped home, the drawer front and back should be parallel, as should the sides. It's wise to fit the assembly into the base drawer opening at this point to check its width for fit.

Making the drawer bottom

The seven-piece drawer bottom is made of two ⁵⁄₁₆-in.-thick panels set into grooves in the five ½-in.-thick frame members. The top faces of all the pieces are flush to each other to create a level surface for the display objects.

1. Dimension the stock for the frame members. Cut them to the finished sizes—with the following exceptions: Make the front and back frame members 1 in. or so longer. Also make the side frame members about ¹⁄₁₆ in. wider.

You'll trim them to final size after assembling the drawer bottom. While you're at it, it's a good idea to cut a bit of extra frame and panel stock for test fitting.

2. Dimension the stock for the floating panels. Book-matching the panels by resawing them from the same piece of stock can create a lovely visual balance.

3. Rout the ³⁄₁₆-in. by ½-in. grooves for the floating panels, as shown in "Drawer Bottom Joinery." The 22¼-in.-long grooves in the front and back frame members are stopped, so you'll have to mark their beginning and end locations first, as shown in the "Drawer Bottom Elevation."

4. Because the frame members are oversize in length, mark out the stopped grooves by measuring from the center to the ends of the frame member.

5. Cut the ³⁄₁₆-in. by ½-in. tenons on the ends of the center frame member on the table saw, sawing the shoulders first (see **photo E**).

6. Cut the cheeks using a tenoning jig (see **photo F**). I saw the cheeks a bit fat, then trim them with a rabbet plane for an exact fit in the groove.

7. Cut the ⅛-in. by ⅜-in. rabbets on the top edges of the floating panels. These can either be sawn on the table saw or routed.

8. Cut the biscuit slots. To lay them out, dry-fit the drawer bottom parts together, then mark for the biscuit locations.

Photo F: The second step in cutting the tenon is to cut the cheeks using a tenoning jig.

9. Fine-tune the fit of the floating panels, which will ride unglued in their grooves. If you're building during a humid summer day, the panels can fit tightly side to side, because they will shrink later during dry, heated winter days in the house. If you're building during conditions of low humidity, take about 1/16 in. off each of the panels' long edges so they will have room to expand during more humid weather.

10. Dry-assemble the drawer bottom in preparation for glue-up. Make sure everything fits well and then rehearse your clamping procedures.

11. Glue up the frame, leaving the floating panels unglued to allow them to expand and contract. Make sure that the bottom is flat under clamping pressure. Also check that the assembly is square after clamping by comparing diagonal measurements made across the interior corners of the outer frame.

Fitting and assembling the drawer

1. Crosscut the bottom to its final length (see "Drawer Bottom Elevation" p. 106). Make sure to cut equal amounts off of each side. To ensure that the bottom is cut squarely, crosscut it using a panel-cutting jig (see "A Panel-Cutting Jig" p. 70).

2. Plane the top surface of the entire bottom to level the frame and floating panels with a jointer plane (see **photo G**).

3. Rabbet the bottom's edges to fit into the grooves in the drawer sides.

If your drawer bottom has remained a fairly consistent thickness even after planing, you can use a rabbeting bit in the router to cut the rabbet. However, if the bottom varies in thickness, the rabbet will too, making a good fit in the grooves difficult. Instead of routing, you can cut the rabbet on the table saw, holding the bottom on edge, with its top pressed against the rip fence, to create a tongue of consistent thickness.

4. Dry-assemble the drawer, fitting the bottom into its grooves (see **photo H**). Make sure that all fits well when the drawer box dovetails are tapped home and that the drawer will clamp up squarely. Definitely rehearse your clamping procedures, because you're going to have to work quickly during the glue-up.

Photo G: Plane the top surface of the drawer bottom to ensure that the panels and frame members are flush.

Photo H: Dry-fit the bottom into the grooves in the drawer front, back, and sides to check the fit before gluing up the drawer.

5. Glue up the drawer, spreading ample glue on the dovetail joints for one side of the drawer. Tap the joints home.

6. Then spread glue sparingly into the grooves, insert the panel, and glue up the dovetail joints on the other side of the drawer. If your dovetails fit reasonably well, you won't have to clamp the drawer. But make sure that it is square, and that it's sitting on a flat surface as it dries.

Fitting the drawer to its opening

1. Plane the top and bottom edges of the drawer box with a sharp jack plane or smoothing plane to remove any saw marks.

2. Use spring clamps to temporarily clamp the back end of the drawer runners to the side aprons. Slide the drawer box into its opening and adjust the runners so that they both contact the drawer bottom along their entire length. Remove the drawer and screw the runners in place at the back.

3. Reinsert the drawer and clamp the drawer front/false apron to the drawer box to check

its fit. To maintain the illusion of the false apron, its ends should fit against the legs with just a hair's clearance.

4. Glue the drawer front/false apron to the drawer box, carefully aligning its top edge with the tops of the adjoining legs. You could instead screw the false apron on from the inside of the drawer, but you would see the screws through the glass top.

FINISHING UP

1. Attach the top by screwing it on from underneath through the cleats. Make sure to balance the overhang all around the base.

2. Apply your favorite finish to all of the exterior surfaces. McDonald used shellac for the entire table, including the drawer. Whatever finish you use for the outside surfaces, it's wise to use shellac for the drawer, because it won't bleed or leave an odor inside.

3. Clean both sides of the glass and lightly drop in place while wearing cotton gloves.

Arts and Crafts Coffee Table

California woodworker John Lavine places great importance on craftsmanship, sturdy construction, and grain composition. That attitude has produced some very fine pieces, including this coffee table.

This table is unconventional and compelling. The double legs at each corner immediately set the table apart from most, but there are many other thoughtful touches as well. The tabletop's lacewood veneer provides a striking complement to its mahogany frame, which is set off by a black inlaid border. The border extends into decorative squares at each corner, conferring a classic touch to this very contemporary piece. The tabletop's edges bevel upward slightly, providing a visual "lift." The shelf provides visual balance, a platform for books and magazines, and great structural integrity.

The table is easier to make than it appears. The top is simply a veneered 1-in.-thick medium-density fiberboard (MDF) panel framed with solid wood. Lavine sawed his own veneers, but you could use commercial veneers instead. The panel on his table was joined with biscuits to the frame, but I chose to use splines here, although I did use biscuits in the mitered joints.

For the inlay, Lavine used color-impregnated wood sold under the trade name Ebon-X. Unfortunately it's hard to find these days. You could use ebony instead or wenge, another blackish wood that is less expensive than ebony or dyed veneer.

Arts and Crafts Coffee Table

THE TOP OF THIS COFFEE TABLE consists of a solid-wood frame glued to a veneered 1" thick MDF panel. Splines and biscuits help align and reinforce the joints. The border inlay strips are inset into the edge of the frame members before gluing the frame to the panel. The base consists of four leg-and-apron assemblies that intersect each other at half-lapped notches. The legs are glued to the aprons with "floating" tenons and screwed unglued to the shelf.

TOP

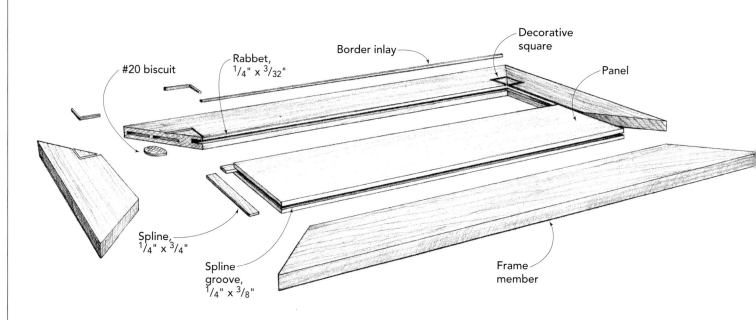

#20 biscuit

Rabbet, $^1/_4$" x $^3/_{32}$"

Border inlay

Decorative square

Panel

Spline, $^1/_4$" x $^3/_4$"

Spline groove, $^1/_4$" x $^3/_8$"

Frame member

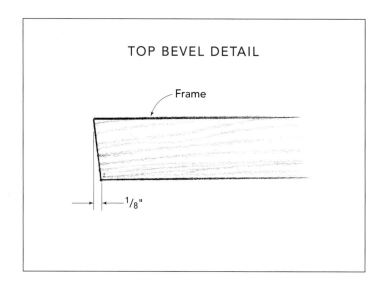

TOP BEVEL DETAIL

Frame

$^1/_8$"

BASE

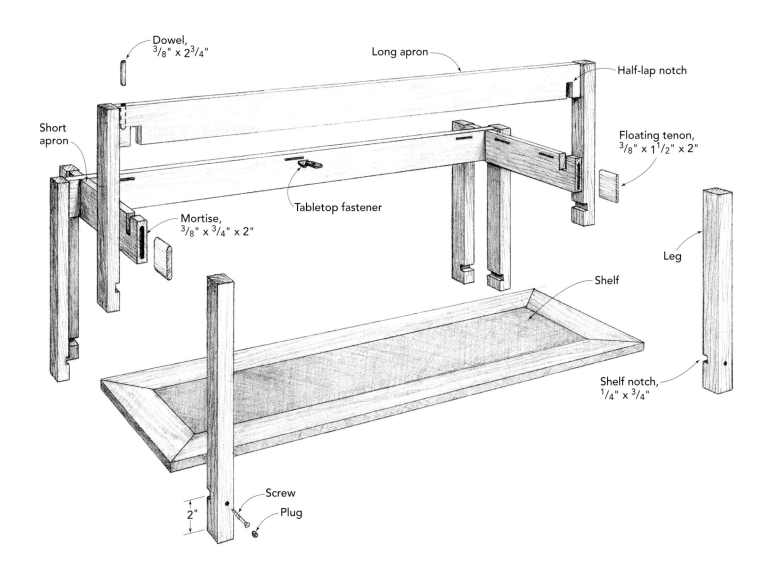

Dowel,
$3/8" \times 2^3/4"$

Long apron

Half-lap notch

Short apron

Floating tenon,
$3/8" \times 1^1/2" \times 2"$

Tabletop fastener

Mortise,
$3/8" \times 3/4" \times 2"$

Leg

Shelf

Shelf notch,
$1/4" \times 3/4"$

Screw

Plug

2"

BUILDING THE TABLE STEP-BY-STEP

CUT LIST FOR ARTS AND CRAFTS COFFEE TABLE		
Top		
2	Frame members	1⅛ in. x 6 in. x 22 in.
2	Frame members	1⅛ in. x 6 in. x 51 in.
1	MDF panel	1 in. x 10 in. x 39 in.
Shelf		
2	Frame members	¾ in. x 2 in. x 14 in.
2	Frame members	¾ in. x 2 in. x 43 in.
1	Hardwood plywood panel	¾ in. x 10 in. x 39 in.
Base		
2	Short aprons	¾ in. x 3 in. x 13½ in.
2	Long aprons	¾ in. x 3 in. x 42½ in.
8	Legs	1¼ in. x 1¼ in. x 14⅞ in.
8	Floating tenons	⅜ in. x 1½ in. x 2 in.
Miscellaneous		
	Spline stock	¼ in. x ¾ in. (fit to length)
	Inlay strips	¼ in. x ⅛ in. (fit to length)

THE TABLE CONSISTS OF three basic parts: the top, the shelf, and the base assembly. The top and shelf are of similar construction, so build them at the same time. Then make the base, which attaches to the shelf.

MAKING THE TOP AND SHELF

Cutting the pieces to size

1. Dimension the frame members for the top and shelf, cutting the pieces a bit long for now. You'll cut them to final length later,

when mitering the corners to fit. It's also best to thickness the shelf frame members to about ¹³⁄₃₂-in., so you can plane them flush to the ¾-in.-thick shelf later.

2. Cut the MDF substrate for the top slightly oversize and veneer it.

3. Saw the top panel to the finished size.

4. Cut the hardwood plywood for the shelf to finished size right off the bat.

Installing the inlay border

1. Rout the ¼-in.-wide by ³⁄₃₂-in.-deep rabbit along all inside edges of the top frame members for the border inlay.

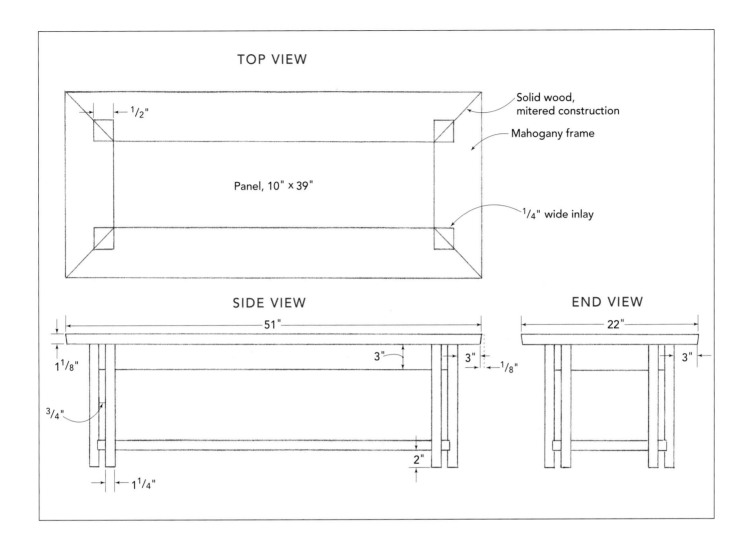

TOP VIEW

Solid wood, mitered construction

Mahogany frame

1/2"

Panel, 10" × 39"

1/4" wide inlay

SIDE VIEW

51"

1 1/8"

3"

3"

1/8"

3/4"

2"

1 1/4"

END VIEW

22"

3"

2. Saw the ¼-in. by ⅛-in. inlay strips. Make extra for the decorative squares that will be inlayed into the corners of the frame later.
3. Glue the inlay strips into the rabbets on the frame members. You can use masking tape to clamp it in place. After the glue dries, plane the inlay flush to the edges and tops of the frame members.

Making the frame joints

1. Rout or saw a ¼-in.-wide by ½-in.-deep spline groove in the edges of the top and shelf panels. A ¼-in. slot-cutting router bit does a quick, accurate job of cutting the grooves.
2. Cut matching grooves in the frame members so that the frame sits about 1/64 in. proud of the panel after assembly.

3. Rip stock for the splines slightly fat, then plane it to final thickness. The splines should fit snugly, requiring just a bit of finger pressure to push them into their grooves. There's no need to miter them at their corners. You can just butt them, as shown.
4. Cut the frame miters on a table saw sled, as shown in **photo A** on p. 117. See "A Table Saw Miter Sled" on p. 116.
5. Fit a pair of miters at one corner of the frame.
6. Work your way around the frame, carefully marking and cutting the miter on the opposite end of each frame member. As you do this, make sure that the frame members are pulled up tightly against the panel.
7. When the frame pieces fit well, mark them for two #20 biscuits per miter joint and cut the biscuit slots.

A TABLE SAW MITER SLED

This shop-built table saw sled allows you to cut miters quickly and accurately on your table saw. The beauty of this system is that, even if the two fences on the sled aren't positioned at exactly 45 degrees to the blade, you're still assured of a square joint, as long as the fences are square to each other.

1. Cut a piece of ¾-in.-thick hardwood plywood to about 20 in. by 30 in.
2. Mill a couple of 24-in.-long hardwood runners to fit in your table saw's miter gauge slots.
3. Place the runners in the miter gauge slots and set your table saw's rip fence about 15 in. to the right of the blade.
4. Run a bead of glue on each runner, then set the panel on top of them, butting its right-hand edge against the rip fence.
5. Screw the plywood to the runners.
6. After the glue dries, place the runners back in the miter gauge slots and saw about 11 in. into the panel.
7. To make the fences, rip two 3-in.-wide strips of plywood, making sure that the edges are straight.
8. Miter one end of each.
9. Attach one fence with screws about 8-in. back from the front of the panel and at 45 degrees to the slot you cut.
10. Lay an accurate square against the attached fence, position the second fence along the opposite leg of the square, then screw the second fence to the panel.
11. Attach a thick block of wood behind the juncture of the fences to shield the blade at the end of a cut.
12. To allow easy retrieval of the sled after a cut, attach a Shaker peg or length of dowel at the rear end of the panel.

TABLE SAW MITER SLED

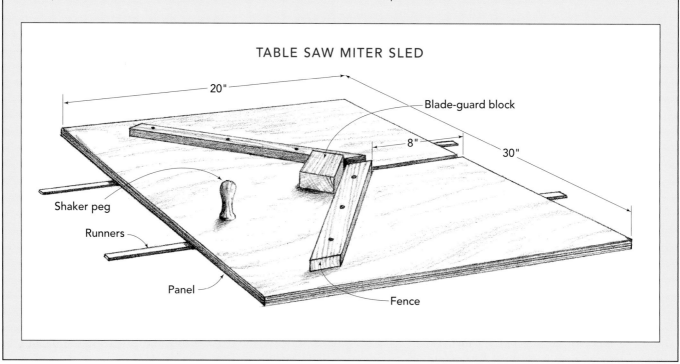

20"

Blade-guard block

8"

30"

Shaker peg

Runners

Panel

Fence

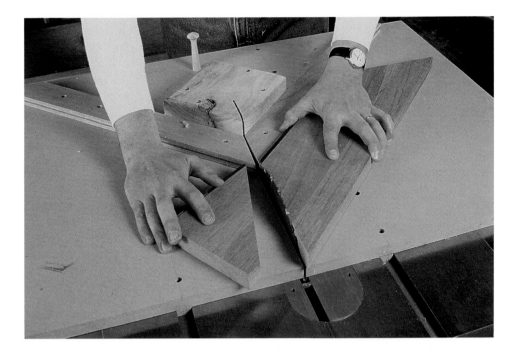

Photo A: A table saw miter sled makes quick, accurate work of sawing the miters for the top and shelf frames.

Assembling the parts

1. Dry-fit the top and shelf panel assemblies with their splines and biscuits to make sure that all of the joints mate well and close up with no problems (see **photo B**).

Make certain that the panel doesn't sit proud of the frame. The thin veneer on the panels won't allow you to plane them flush with the frame later. This dry-assembly is also a good opportunity to rehearse your clamping procedures.

2. Glue up the top and shelf assemblies. I suggest using white glue for this because it allows a longer setting time than does yellow glue and there's a lot to glue up at once. Have all your clamps, glue brushes, and so on, at hand before you start.

3. Apply glue to the spline grooves, the splines, and all joint faces. A good approach is to glue the short frame members to the panel first, making sure that the inside corners of the miters meet the corners of the panel. Then glue on the long frame members. Use ample glue on the biscuit-joined miters. Make sure

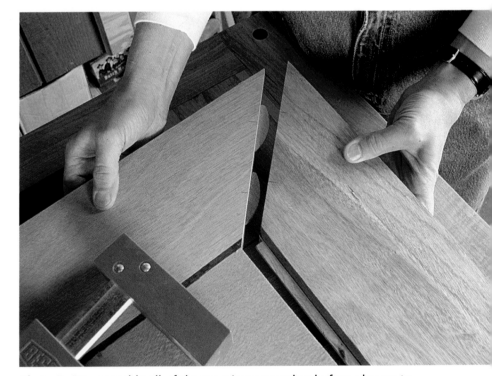

Photo B: Dry-assemble all of the top pieces together before glue-up to make sure they fit tightly.

all the joints line up well under clamp pressure and that the veneered panel doesn't sit proud of the frame members.

4. After the glue is dry, remove the clamps and plane and scrape the frames flush to the panels (see **photo C**). Take care not to cut through the veneer.

5. Plane the edges of the top, making sure they meet neatly at the tips of the miters. Then plane a ⅛-in. upward taper on the edges of the top.

6. Lightly "break" the sharp edges on the top and shelf with 150-grit sandpaper.

Inlaying the decorative squares

1. Carefully lay out the lines for the 2½-in.-square corner inlays on the top. Using an accurate square, mark the lines lightly with a sharp pencil (see **photo D**). Go over the lines with a knife, making sure that they meet neatly at the corners.

2. Deepen the knife lines using a wide chisel (see **photo E**).

Photo C: Use a smoothing plane to level the frame to the panel. To prevent planing through the thin veneer, use a sharp scraper for your final passes.

Photo D: Lay out the decorative squares at the corners of the tabletop using an accurate square and a sharp pencil. Then deepen the lines with a knife.

Photo E: To cut the inlay grooves by hand, begin by carefully chopping the walls of the grooves with a sharp chisel set in your knifed lines.

3. Cut the inlay grooves. Although you can use a router guided by a straightedge for this, I prefer to cut them by hand with a chisel and sharp router plane.

4. Plane out the waste between the lines with a router plane (see **photo F**). Use a ¼-in.-wide cutter, lowering it for each subsequent pass until you reach the final ³⁄₃₂-in. depth.

5. Cut the inlay pieces to length to fit the grooves, then glue them into the grooves, lightly tapping them into place with a hammer (see **photo G**).

Photo F: Using a router plane fitted with a sharp ¼-in.-wide blade, plane out the waste between the groove walls. Take light passes, adjusting the blade downward as you go.

Photo G: Apply the inlay strips into the groove, fitting and gluing one piece at a time to ensure tight butt joints.

Photo H: Use a
smoothing plane to
cut the inlay flush to
the frame.

6. After the glue dries, use a sharp smoothing plane to level the inlay flush to the frame (see **photo H**).

MAKING THE BASE

The base is really not that complex to build. You'll make the four aprons and eight legs, cut the mortises, make the floating tenons, then cut the shelf notches in the legs. All that's left is to notch the aprons and assemble the base around the shelf.

Making the parts and cutting the apron-to-leg joints

1. Cut the aprons and legs to size.
2. Lay out the ⅜-in. by 2-in. apron mortises, centering them on the ends of the aprons.
3. Lay out the matching mortises on the legs, starting each one ½ in. down from the top of the leg and centered across the leg's width.

4. Rout the mortises using a ⅜-in.-diameter straight or upcut spiral router bit in a router outfitted with an edge guide. Clamp scrap pieces to the workpiece as necessary to provide extra bearing surface for the router. To ensure consistent apron setback, always reference the router fence against the outside face of the aprons.
5. Make the floating tenon stock by ripping it slightly oversize and then planing it to final thickness.
6. Test the fit by inserting the stock into a mortise. It should slide in easily, with just a bit of resistance.
7. Rout a ³⁄₁₆-in. roundover on every edge of the tenon stock to match the ⅜-in. diameter at the end of the mortises (see **photo I**). This is most easily and safely done on a router table. Then cut the tenons to length.
8. Using a marking knife, lay out the half-lap joints where the aprons cross each other. But don't cut them yet. Lay the lines out accurately so that the edges of the aprons will meet flush when joined.
9. Install ⅜-in.-diameter by 2¾-in.-long dowels into the top edge of the aprons. The glued dowels help strengthen the short-grain area between the notch and the mortise. The dowel center should be in ¼ in. from the end of each apron.
10. Lay out and cut the notches in the legs to accept the shelf. You can do this with a dado head on the table saw or with a handsaw and chisel.
11. Drill for the #6 by 1⅝-in. drywall screws that will hold the legs in the notches. Then counterbore the holes to accept wooden plugs.

Assembling the base

The base assembly is a bit of a Chinese puzzle. For everything to fit, you'll need to assemble the aprons, legs, and shelf in the following specific sequence. Use white glue for a longer open-assembly time and work on a flat surface. Definitely dry-assemble and do a clamping rehearsal in every case before you reach for the glue bottle.

Photo I: After rounding over the edges of the tenon stock and cutting the tenons to length, dry-assemble the leg-to-apron joints. The tenons should fit in the mortise snugly, requiring only a bit of finger pressure to insert them.

1. Glue up the two long apron/leg assemblies. Work on a flat surface and make sure each assembly is flat and square under clamp pressure. Let dry thoroughly.

2. Now is the time to cut out the half-lap notches on the long aprons. If you had cut them before assembling the apron/leg unit, clamping pressure might have broken the short-grain section next to the notch.

3. Cut the notch shoulder. I use a bowsaw. Then chisel out the waste (see **photo J**).

4. Cut the notches on the short aprons, making sure that they slip tightly over the long aprons. This way, the short-grain sections are backed up by the long aprons during glue-up.

5. Double-check to make sure that the edges of the dry-fit aprons are flush, or the legs won't sit properly after assembly.

6. Make tick marks on the underside of the shelf to reference the position of all the legs. Each leg sits in 1-in. from the corner of the shelf.

7. Working on a low bench, lay one long apron/leg assembly down flat and insert the shelf fully into the leg notches.

Photo J: After gluing up the long apron and leg assemblies, cut the half-lap notches in all of the aprons.

BASE ASSEMBLY

Because the shelf sits captured between notches in the legs, the base assembly is a bit like a Chinese puzzle. The parts must be assembled in the sequence shown here.

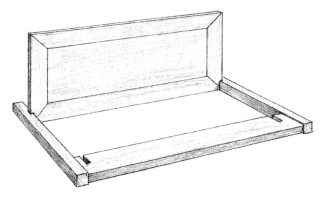

1. Insert the shelf into one long apron/leg assembly; do not use glue.

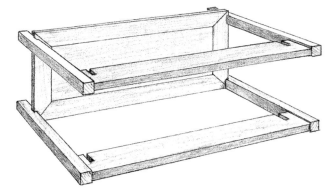

2. Slip the second long apron/leg assembly onto the shelf.

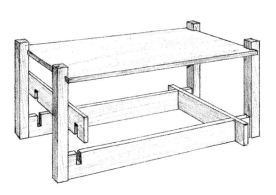

3. Glue the short aprons into the notches on long aprons.

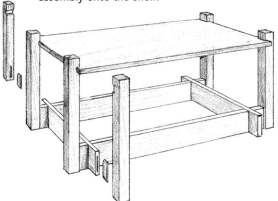

4. Glue the legs to the short aprons. Screw all the legs to the shelf; do not use glue. Finally, plug the screw holes.

8. Slip the opposite apron/leg assembly onto the shelf, as shown in "Base Assembly."

9. Stand the base upside down and align the legs with the tick marks you made earlier.

10. Apply glue to the bottoms of the notches, slip the short aprons into the notches on the long aprons, and clamp them in place. Again, make sure that the top edges of the long and short aprons are flush.

11. Glue the legs to the short aprons, but not to the shelf. Use just enough clamping pressure to pull the joints snug. If your half-lap

joints are tight, the short grain should have enough support to prevent breaking, but don't tempt fate by cranking down the clamps. Make sure the tops of the legs are flush to the top edges of the aprons.

12. Align each leg to its tick mark and attach it to the shelf with a $1\frac{5}{8}$-in.-long drywall screw. Drilling a pilot hole into the shelf first will prevent it from splitting.

13. Glue wood plugs into the counterbored holes. Lavine used black plugs, which serve as design accents. Alternatively, you could make

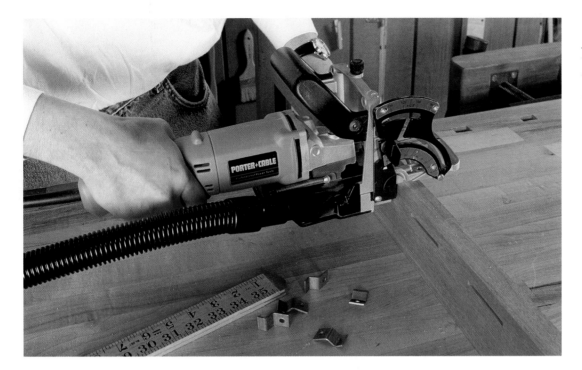

a nearly invisible joint by using a plug of the same wood as the leg, orienting the grain of each in the same direction. When the glue is dry, trim the plugs flush.

ATTACHING THE TOP

The top is held in place with S-shaped metal tabletop fasteners, available through many woodworking supply catalogs. One end of the fastener is screwed into the tabletop and the other end fits into a slot cut in the apron.

1. Place the tabletop upside down on the bench and then center the base on it. Position a tabletop fastener on the underside of the top and measure the necessary offset for the apron slots.

2. Stand the base upright and cut the fastener slots in the aprons. I use a biscuit joiner for this (see **photo K**). Three or four slots in each long apron and a couple each in the short aprons are plenty.

3. Place the base upside down on the table-top again. Insert the fasteners into the biscuit slots.

4. Mark the locations for the screws in the underside of the top, then drill pilot holes and install the screws.

FINISHING UP

Lavine used several coats of lacquer to finish his table. Lacquer imparts a wonderful depth and subtle gloss to the fine woods and inlay work on this table. Unfortunately for many small shops, lacquer must be sprayed. It can also be highly flammable, so it must be applied either outdoors or in a spray booth equipped with explosion-proof lights and venting. If you want a lacquer finish and you're not equipped to spray it, consider taking the table to a professional finisher.

Another good option for bringing out the depth of these woods is to apply several coats of oil. You can use tung oil, Danish oil, or boiled linseed oil (see "Boiled Linseed Oil Finish" on p. 137). Tung oil darkens wood less than do linseed and Danish oils.

Classic Console Table

I made this half-round classic console table for my home. I designed it more for looks than utility, although it does provide a lovely platform for a decorative object or vase of flowers. Because of its half-round shape and its lovely mahogany and walnut woods, the table looks rather formal and dignified.

This design embodies several important characteristics I value in furniture: visual simplicity, structural integrity, and function. It's actually a deceptively simple design. The table sports no intricate edge details, inlay, or beading. The only extra touches here are the chamfer on the underside of the top, and the apron moldings, which balance and accentuate the overlap of the top.

Although light in appearance and weight, the table is very strong. The curved apron connects to the legs with large mortise-and-tenon joints. Half-lap dovetails on the rear rail lock into sockets on the rear legs, creating a strong, triangulated assembly. The top, reinforces the whole structure.

Building this half-round table is not difficult. The top curve is easily cut with a jigsaw and the legs involve very basic turning techniques. Making the curved apron blanks is an easy matter of gluing and clamping thin laminations between a shopmade bending form. The only tricky construction involves the layout, cutting, and fitting of the apron tenons. To help you, I've provided a pattern for marking the joints and aligning the parts for assembly.

Classic Console Table

THIS LITTLE HALF-ROUND TABLE is not as complicated to build as you might think. The curved top is simply cut to shape with a jigsaw, then the legs are turned and mortised. The curved aprons are made from thin laminations glued together in a shopmade bending form. The only tricky part is fitting the tenon, and that is simplified by the use of a full-scale pattern.

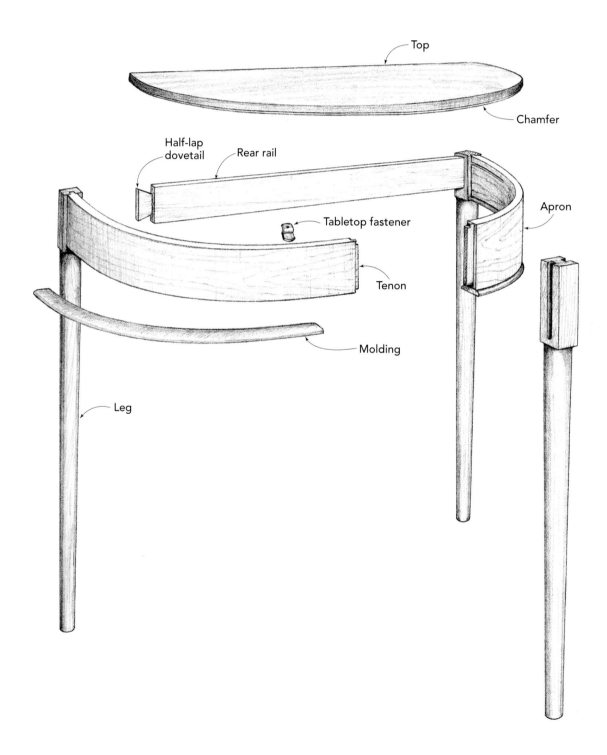

Top

Chamfer

Half-lap
dovetail

Rear rail

Apron

Tabletop fastener

Tenon

Molding

Leg

CLASSIC CONSOLE TABLE PATTERN

Draw this pattern to full scale and use it as a reference
for sizing parts, laying out joints, and assembling the base.

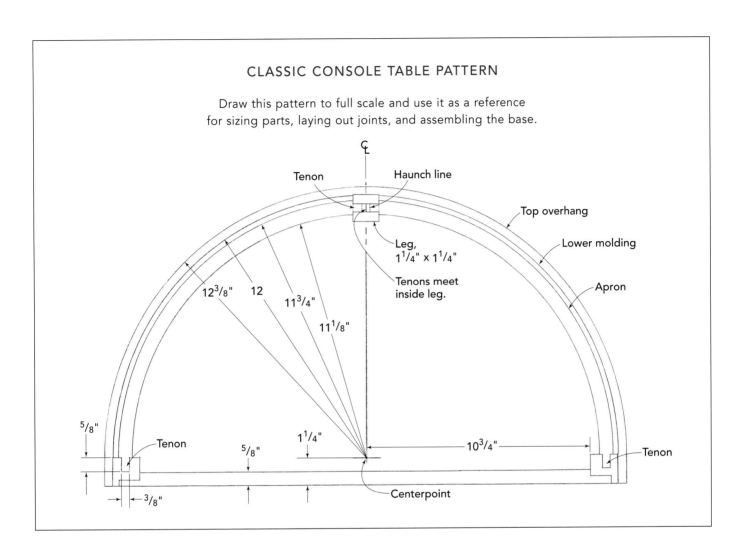

CUT LIST FOR CLASSIC CONSOLE TABLE

Top		
1	Cutting blank	⅝ in. x 14 in. x 26 in.
Base		
3	Legs	1¼ in. x 1¼ in. x 25⅝ in.
10	Apron laminations	⅛ in. x 3¼ in. x 25 in.
1	Rear rail	⅝ in. x 2 in. x 25 in. (Mark to final length at assembly.)
1	Molding trim blank	¼ in. x 6 in. x 18 in.

BUILDING THE TABLE STEP-BY-STEP

THE MAIN INGREDIENTS of the table are a top, two curved apron pieces, a rear rail, and three legs. Bullnose molding strips attach to the bottom of the curved aprons. The first thing you'll need to make is the full-scale pattern, which you'll use as a working reference. Next, you'll turn the legs and cut their mortises. Then you'll make the two curved apron pieces, join them to the legs, and apply the molding strips.

MAKING THE TOP

1. Begin by making a full-scale pattern, using the "Classic Console Table Pattern" (see p. 127). Use a trammel to lay out the curved sections. Notice that the circle center point is in line with the front edges of the rear legs.

2. Make a 14-in. by 26-in. blank by thicknessing boards to ⅝ in., jointing their edges, then gluing them together. Make sure the panel glues up flat. When the glue dries, plane and scrape the blank smooth.

3. Using the "Classic Console Table Pattern" as a reference, set trammel points on a beam to match the radius of the top. Then draw the arc on your blank. Locate the trammel swing point 1½ in. in from the edge of the blank. This will create a temporary ¼-in. overhang at the rear of the tabletop, which you may need when adjusting the top to fit the base, as explained later.

4. Cut the top to shape. Because a piece of this size can be difficult to maneuver on the bandsaw, I cut the shape with a jigsaw (see **photo A**).

Photo A: Use a jigsaw to cut the half-round top from the blank.

Photo B: After routing the chamfer on the underside of the top, use a ⅛-in. roundover bit on the top side.

EDGING AND OFFSET DETAILS

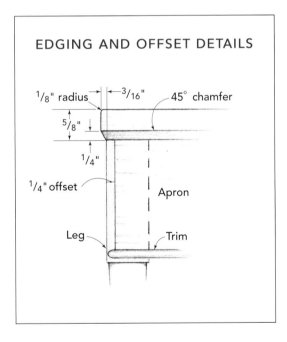

¹/₈" radius   ←—³/₁₆"   45° chamfer

⁵/₈"

¹/₄"

¹/₄" offset

Apron

Leg   Trim

5. Smooth the curved edge with a spoke-shave, rasp, wood file, or orbital block sander.
6. Clamp the top to the bench upside down and rout a chamfer on the underside of the curved edge, as shown in "Edging and Offset Details."
7. Break the front edge of the chamfer very slightly with 220-grit sandpaper.
8. Rout a ⅛-in. radius on the top edge (see **photo B**). If you don't have a ⅛-in.-diameter roundover bit, you can create the roundover with an orbital block sander.

MAKING THE LEGS

The turned legs have a square section at the top where the apron pieces meet them. Below that, the legs are turned, tapering in diameter from 1 ³⁄₁₆-in. at the top to ¾-in. at the foot, as shown in "Leg Detail" (see p. 130). I turn the legs first, then cut them to final length before laying out and cutting the mortises at the top.

Photo C: Using a skew chisel, make a cut 3½ in. down from the top of the leg to cleanly define the bottom of the square section.

Turning the shape

1. Dimension stock to 1¼ in. square to make the leg blanks.

2. Cut the blanks to about 30 in. in length, then mark the turning centers on each end. Mark these accurately so the square section of the leg will not appear off-center on the finished leg.

3. Mount a blank in the lathe. Make V-cuts to establish the top and bottom of the leg.

4. Make a V-cut with a skew chisel to define the lower end of the square section. Do this carefully and deftly, because the cut will be very noticeable on the finished table (see **photo C**).

Photo D: Begin shaping the leg by turning it to a cylinder with a roughing gouge.

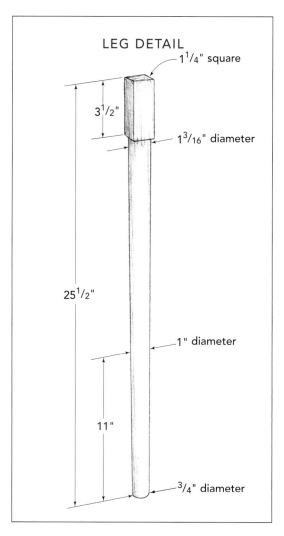

LEG DETAIL

1¼" square

3½"

1³⁄₁₆" diameter

25½"

1" diameter

11"

³⁄₄" diameter

5. Use a roughing gouge to turn the rest of the leg to a cylinder (see **photo D**).

6. Use a parting tool and calipers to establish a 1-in.-diameter reference cut 11 in. up from the foot (see **photo E**).

7. Use a skew chisel to turn the taper. Check your progress occasionally with calipers (see **photo F**).

8. When you've completed the taper, sand it while the leg is spinning on the lathe.

Cutting the mortises

1. On the square sections of the legs, lay out the mortises to accept the haunched tenons, as shown in "Apron Tenon Detail." Centering the mortises across the thickness of the leg will create the desired ¼-in. offset for the apron.

Photo E: Cut a 1-in.-diameter groove 11 in. up from the foot to establish a midpoint reference for turning the leg's taper.

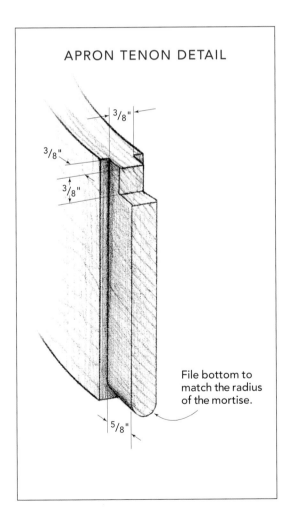

APRON TENON DETAIL

3/8"

3/8"

3/8"

File bottom to match the radius of the mortise.

5/8"

Photo F: Turn the taper with a skew chisel. Use calipers to check the 1³⁄₁₆-in. diameter at the top of the taper and the ¾-in. diameter at the foot.

Photo G: To rout the mortises, I wedge the leg into a U-shaped cradle, aligning the joint face to the top edge of the jig, which supports the router. A router edge guide rides against the wall of the jig.

2. Rout the mortises. I wedge each leg into a shopmade, U-shaped router cradle to hold it for cutting. The router edge guide follows the outside wall of the cradle to guide the cut (see **photo G**). The mortises for the middle leg will meet in the center of the leg.

MAKING THE APRON

The apron consists of two curved sections that are made by gluing and clamping thin strips of wood between a two-part, shopmade bending form. The rails attach to the legs with mortise-and-tenon joints. The rear rail is dovetailed to the rear legs to tie the whole assembly together. Curved molding applied to the bottom edges completes the table base.

Making the bending forms

1. Using a drawing trammel, lay out three two-part bending form pieces on inexpensive ¾-in.-thick plywood. A 9-in.-radius arc defines the inside edge of each form piece, and an 11¾-in.-radius arc defines the outside edge, as shown in "Making the Bending Forms." The arcs should span about a third of a circle.
2. Outfit your router with a ⅝-in.-diameter straight bit and a trammel base (see "Shopmade Router Trammel" on p. 22).
3. Position the router trammel's pivot point 11⅛ in. from the near edge of the bit and screw the trammel to the workpiece. Now through rout a ⅝-in.-wide slot to divide each form into an inner and outer piece.
4. Repeat for the remaining form pieces.
5. Use a jigsaw to cut each half-form to final shape.
6. Stack the inner and outer forms, gluing and nailing plywood blocking between the form pieces. Take care to align the routed edges of the forms as you build them. And make sure to set the blocking back a bit from the edges of the form pieces.
7. Apply a couple coats of polyurethane and wax to the clamping platform and to the tops and mating faces of the forms so glue won't stick to them.

Laminating the apron pieces

1. Mill the ⅛-in.-thick stock for the apron laminates. Resaw or rip the pieces from stock about 3¼ in. wide by about 25 in. long. I saw the pieces about ⁵⁄₃₂ in. thick, then plane ¹⁄₆₄ in. off each side in my thickness planer.
2. Dry-clamp the pieces in the form to preset your clamps and to rehearse your clamping procedure.
3. Align the edges of the laminates and place them between the forms.
4. Squeeze the forms together at the center with a bar clamp, cranking it down as far as the clamp's screw will allow. Then finish

Making the Bending Forms

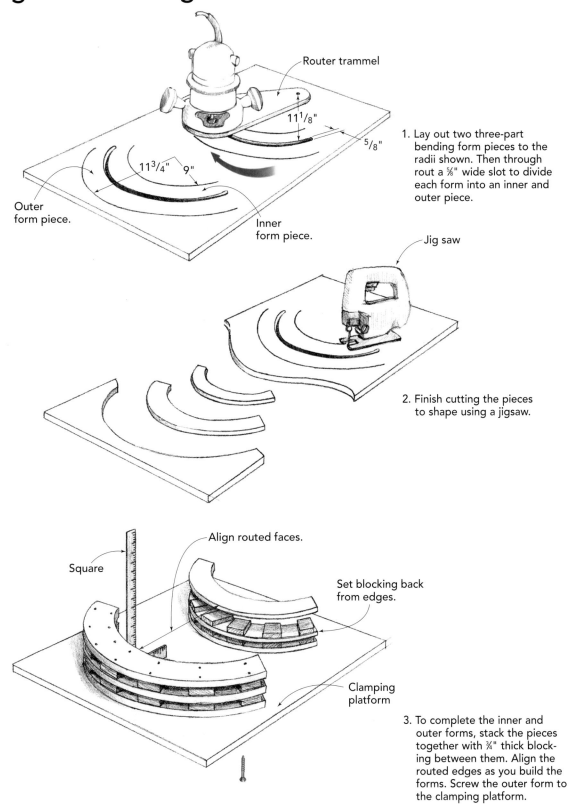

Router trammel

$11\frac{1}{8}$"

$5\frac{}{8}$"

$11\frac{3}{4}$" 9"

Outer
form piece.

Inner
form piece.

1. Lay out two three-part
   bending form pieces to the
   radii shown. Then through
   rout a ⅝" wide slot to divide
   each form into an inner and
   outer piece.

Jig saw

2. Finish cutting the pieces
   to shape using a jigsaw.

Align routed faces.

Square

Set blocking back
from edges.

Clamping
platform

3. To complete the inner and
   outer forms, stack the pieces
   together with ¾" thick blocking between them. Align the
   routed edges as you build the
   forms. Screw the outer form to
   the clamping platform.

Photo H: Use two bar clamps, working them in tandem, to squeeze the apron laminations between the two forms.

Photo I: Clamp with handscrews alongside the bar clamps because of their wide bearing surface. Then remove the bar clamps.

squeezing the forms together with a second clamp (see **photo H**).

5. I use handscrews for the final clamping, because their long jaws provide bearing fully across the faces of the forms. Begin by clamping alongside the bar clamps and then work outward toward the ends of the forms (see **photo I**).

6. After you've rehearsed the clamping, glue up the apron pieces one at a time. I use a small foam paint roller to spread glue on all but the outside faces of the outer laminations (see **photo J**). Spread the glue evenly, but don't overdo it. You don't want glue squeezing out all over the forms.

7. Clamp the laminations into the forms as you did during your rehearsal. Make sure that the handscrews are exerting pressure at both the bottom and the top of the laminations.

Completing the curved aprons

1. Scrape the glue squeeze-out from one edge of each apron piece, then plane that edge smooth and flat.

Photo J: Spread a thin, even coat of glue onto the apron laminations using a foam paint roller. Coat all but the innermost and outermost faces of the laminations.

2. Rip each piece to 3 in. wide on the table saw. I set the blade about 2 in. high and work carefully and slowly. Keep the planed side of the piece tight to the rip fence as you feed the piece past the blade. Use a push stick as you approach the end of the cut. For additional control, you can clamp a curved block to the fence to help guide the workpiece.

3. Plane away the saw marks on the edge you just cut.

4. Lay one apron piece in place on the pattern, distributing the excess length evenly. Because of the typical "springback" of curved laminations, the workpiece curve won't match the pattern exactly. That's okay.

5. Keeping the workpiece centered lengthwise on the pattern, pull the last few inches of the apron in line with the pattern. Draw tick marks on the workpiece to locate the front and back tenon shoulders and the end of the tenon. Mark out the remaining tenons in the same manner.

6. Extend the tick marks across the inner and outer faces of each apron piece using a square.

Then connect each inner and outer line by drawing a line across the edges of the stock.

7. Clamp each workpiece in a vise and cross-cut the ends to length.

8. Mark out the tenon cheek lines on the edges and ends of each workpiece. Then carefully center them across the thickness of the apron stock.

9. Cut the tenons. Saw the shoulders first, slightly undercutting the outer shoulders to ensure a snug fit against the leg. Then saw the cheeks, leaving the tenons a bit fat for now.

10. Use a rabbet plane to trim the tenon cheeks for a snug fit in their mortises. Lay the pieces on the pattern as you work. Because the fit of one joint affects the fit of the others, work them all at once, planing a bit here, then there, until everything fits well and lays out relatively well on the pattern.

11. Trim the shoulders as necessary to bring them in contact with the faces of the legs. The back shoulders may need more trimming than the front shoulders.

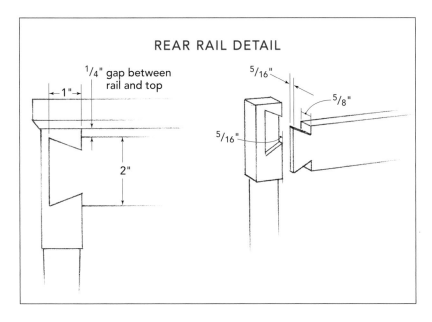

REAR RAIL DETAIL

1/4" gap between rail and top

1"

5/16"

5/8"

5/16"

2"

Photo K: I use a chisel and router plane to cut the socket in the rear legs for the half-lap dovetail on the rear rail.

Fitting the rear rail

1. Dimension stock for the rear rail.
2. Dry-fit the curved aprons to the legs, aligning them on top of the pattern. If the assembly splays outward a bit too much, you can pull the rear legs together slightly with a bar clamp to align the aprons to the pattern. But don't force it. It's okay if everything doesn't line up perfectly; that's to be expected when working with curved forms like this.
3. Place the rear rail against the back of the rear legs and mark for the half-lap dovetail shoulders by tracing along the inside edges of the legs.
4. Lay out and saw the 5/16-in.-thick half-lap dovetails on the rear rail. The angle of the tails isn't critical: 10 or 12 degrees is fine.
5. Remove the rear legs from the assembly and mark them for the dovetail sockets by tracing the outline of the tails. As shown in "Rear Rail Detail," the rail sits 1/4 in. below the top of the legs.
6. Cut the 5/16-in.-deep dovetail sockets. You can use an electric router and chisel the corners afterward, but I prefer to use a router plane and chisel (see **photo K**).

ASSEMBLING THE TABLE AND MAKING THE MOLDING

All of the parts need to be assembled at once, rather than gluing together preassembled sections. You shouldn't need clamps if everything fits right. However, if you need to pull the aprons into the legs a bit, you can clamp handscrews onto the aprons to provide clamping surfaces for bar clamps.

1. Dry-assemble the aprons, legs, and rear rail to make sure everything fits well and to prepare for glue-up. Insert the apron tenons into their mortises and the rear rail into its dovetail sockets.
2. Glue up the assembly, working on a flat surface.
3. Mill a piece of 1/4-in. by 6-in. by 18-in. stock for making the two apron molding strips.

4. Using the pattern to set a trammel, draw the moldings onto your stock. Draw them 1 in. or so longer than the length on the pattern. Then cut them out with a jigsaw or scrollsaw.

5. Fit the pieces to the underside of the apron sections. Hold each one in place against the front of the legs to mark the initial length.

6. Crosscut the pieces at the marks, then trim the ends back bit by bit until the molding projects no less than ¼-in. at any point from the front of the apron. Don't worry if the offset is inconsistent along its length.

7. Glue and nail the moldings in place. After the glue dries, file the edges of the moldings to create a consistent offset.

8. Completely round over the front edges of the molding with sandpaper to create the bullnose profile. An orbital or detail sander works well for this.

9. Cut slots in the curved aprons to accept tabletop fasteners. You can easily rout the slots with a slot-cutter bit. Three slots in each apron piece will do the trick. There's no need for slots in the rear rail.

FINISHING UP

1. To attach the top, first place it upside down on the bench.

2. Place the base upside down on the top. The tabletop overhang probably won't be consistent because of some asymmetry in the base. That's why you built in the extra ¼-in. overhang at the rear of the top. Just position the base to create as consistent a front overhang as possible.

3. Position the top as well as possible, then attach the top to the base with the fasteners. (see **photo L**).

4. Plane the back edge of the top even with the rear rail.

5. Apply your favorite finish. Under no circumstances should you ruin these lovely woods by staining them. Three coats of boiled linseed oil, as described in "Boiled Linseed Oil Finish," will give the table a rich natural glow.

Photo L: Attach the top using tabletop fasteners set into grooves in the curved apron.

BOILED LINSEED OIL FINISH

A boiled linseed oil finish shows off the beauty of the wood, giving it a rich, natural look. I buy boiled—not raw—linseed oil that I heat on a hot plate or a double boiler to the temperature of hot coffee. I apply three coats, 24 hours apart. Using a rag, I flood the surface, let it soak in about 20 minutes, then wipe it off. Because linseed oil can seep during humid weather and can turn rancid inside a case, don't apply it to any interior surfaces, including the underside of the top over the carcase.

Caution: To prevent spontaneous combustion of your finishing rags, spread them flat on the ground outside until they dry.

STURDY KITCHEN TABLE

This cherry kitchen table is my version of one designed and built by Frank Klausz, a well-known professional cabinetmaker and author. The table is a classic, utilitarian design that comfortably seats six. It consists of a top and a very simple, well-proportioned base. But the real stand-out feature of this table is the long bevel on the edges of the top. The detail is lovely, but you don't fully appreciate it until you sit down at the table to eat. When you do, you realize that the bevel matches the angle of your forearms as they rest on the edge, making for a very comfortable dining experience.

Klausz originally designed the table for his own kitchen, but it has proved to be a good seller for him as well. Throughout the years, he has made many similar versions for customers, who often commission it as a wedding present. He's made the tables from various woods, including oak, maple, cherry, and ash—sometimes combining two different woods in one table.

This design is a perfect example of basic, sound, table construction. The top is a solid-wood plank. It sits on a base consisting of four square legs joined to four aprons with mortise-and-tenon joints. The top attaches to the base with "button blocks," which allow the tabletop to expand and contract with seasonal changes in humidity.

Sturdy Kitchen Table

THE TOP OF THIS TABLE is a solid-wood plank, which sits on a base consisting of four square legs and four aprons joined with mortise-and-tenon joints. The top attaches to the base with "button blocks" that allow the tabletop to expand and contract with seasonal changes. The table seats six.

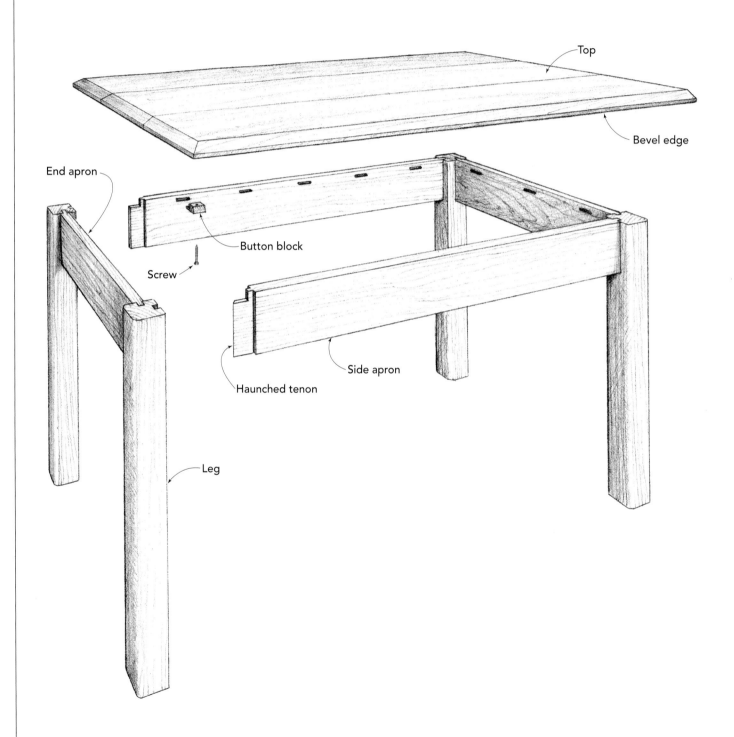

Top

Bevel edge

End apron

Button block

Screw

Haunched tenon

Side apron

Leg

Mortise-and-Tenon Detail

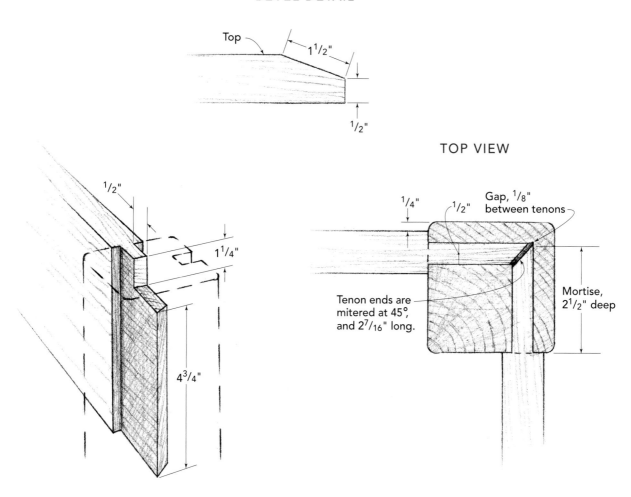

BEVEL DETAIL

Top

$1^{1}/_{2}$"

$^{1}/_{2}$"

$^{1}/_{2}$"

$1^{1}/_{4}$"

$4^{3}/_{4}$"

TOP VIEW

$^{1}/_{4}$"

$^{1}/_{2}$"

Gap, $^{1}/_{8}$"
between tenons

Tenon ends are
mitered at 45°,
and $2^{7}/_{16}$" long.

Mortise,
$2^{1}/_{2}$" deep

CUT LIST FOR STURDY KITCHEN TABLE

Top		
1	Panel	1 in. x 34 in. x 62 in.
Base		
4	Legs	3 in. x 3 in. x 29½ in.
2	Aprons	1 in. x 5 in. x 27⅞ in. (including tenons)
2	Aprons	1 in. x 5 in. x 50⅞ in. (including tenons)
14	Button blocks	¾ in. x 1 in. x 2 in.

BUILDING THE TABLE STEP-BY-STEP

BUILDING THIS TABLE is a great exercise in solid, fundamental woodworking. The top is made by edge-joining boards to make the plank. Making the bevel affords fine practice with a smoothing plane, and making the mortise-and-tenon joints for the base is a lesson in fabricating one of woodworking's strongest and most time-honored joints.

I make the top first, then the base. When making the base, start with the legs because the apron tenons are fit to the leg mortises afterward.

MAKING THE TOP

Making the panel

1. Select your nicest-looking boards for the top. Make sure they are reasonably flat and straight.

2. Joint one face of each, then thickness plane the boards to about 1⅛₆ in. After gluing up the boards, you'll plane the top to 1 in. thick while flattening and smoothing it.

3. Arrange the boards for a pleasing grain match. Klaus likes to use the "inside" faces of boards as the show surface. The inside face is the one that was oriented toward the center of the tree, as indicated by the annular rings on the end of the board. He claims the inside face has more depth and a richer texture. Personally, I'm not that fussy.

4. Once the boards are laid out to your satisfaction, draw a V across them so you can easily reorient them later for glue-up.

5. Joint the edges of the boards. Stock this long could be a problem to joint with a handplane alone, so I first run them across a jointer to do the initial straightening. After running one edge on the jointer, I place that edge against my table saw rip fence and rip

Photo A: I snap a Japanese ink line along the edge of the tabletop to establish a cut line for ripping the edge.

the other edge. Then I run the second edge over the jointer.

6. Place the boards together edge to edge and inspect the joint lines for gaps. If an edge is bellied, take a couple of passes with a jointer plane along its center section to straighten it.

7. Once the edges are straight, "spring" the joints by planing off one or two fine shavings from the center two thirds of each. This should create a gap of about 1/64 in. at the center of the joint, ensuring that the boards meet tightly at their ends.

8. Glue up the top. Place the boards on clamping stands or sawhorses, realigning the V marks that you drew when originally laying them out. Apply glue evenly to the edges and sprinkle a few grains of coarse sand into the glue at the center and ends to keep the boards from slipping out of alignment under clamping pressure.

9. Clamp the boards together, working from the center outward. Begin with light pressure, then monitor the alignment of the boards as you crank down on the clamps. Lightly clamping cauls across the ends of the panel helps keep it flat during glue-up.

10. After the glue has dried for at least 3 hours, remove the clamps and scrape off the excess glue. Then plane the panel to flatten and smooth it to a thickness of 1 in.

11. Stand the panel upright on one edge, clamp it in a bench vise, then plane one edge smooth with a jointer plane.

12. Rip the panel to width on your table saw, holding the planed edge against the rip fence. If your saw is too small to rip a panel this wide, mark the width at each end of the panel, then draw your cut line by connecting the marks with the help of a straightedge. Instead of using a straightedge, I snap the cut line using a Japanese ink line (see **photo A**).

13. Mark the panel to length by drawing a cut line squarely across each end. Then make the cut using a portable circular saw guided by a straightedge. Alternatively, you could make the cut with a handsaw (see **photo B**).

14. Plane or sand the crosscut edges smooth.

Making the bevel

1. Mark for the bevel using a cutting gauge to score two crisp lines all around the edges of the panel. Score one fairly deep line ½ in. up from the bottom of the edge and lightly score the other 1½ in. in from the perimeter. Scored

Photo B: Because the tabletop is too large to crosscut on the table saw, it must be cut to length with a handsaw or portable circular saw. I use a Japanese ryoba saw.

lines will help you better than pencil lines when it comes to gauging the bevel cuts, as you'll see next.

2. Clamp the panel to the benchtop and use a sharp jack plane to cut the bevel.

3. Begin by taking moderately heavy cuts (see **photo C** on p. 144).

4. As you approach your gauge lines, readjust your plane iron for a very fine cut. When

Photo C: Use a smoothing plane to create the bevel on the tabletop. Begin by taking moderately heavy cuts, then adjust the plane iron for a very light cut as you approach the bevel layout lines on the top and sides of the plank.

MAKING THE BASE

Making the legs

Chances are, you may have a problem finding stock thick enough to make the 3-in.-square legs. If so, you'll have to make the leg blanks by laminating thinner stock.

1. To laminate leg stock, rip eight pieces of 8/4 stock to about 3½ in. wide. Crosscut each to about 32 in. long and joint one face of each piece.

2. Glue the pieces together in pairs, spreading a thin, even coat of glue on the jointed faces (see **photo D**). I drop just a few grains of coarse sand into the glue at the ends and center of the pieces to help keep them aligned under clamp pressure.

3. Start by clamping the pieces together with moderate pressure (see **photo E**). Work from the center outward, positioning the clamps about 5 in. apart on every edge.

4. When they're all placed, tighten them down, again working outward from the center. I work on clamping stands to allow easy clamp access.

5. When the glue is dry, dress the stock to the leg sizes.

6. Crosscut the legs to length on the table saw, guiding the workpiece with the miter gauge (see **photo F** on p. 146).

7. Lay out the ½-in. by 5-in. mortises on the two inside faces of each leg. Don't forget to account for the ¼-in. apron offset. Draw a line to indicate the length of the ½-in.-long haunched area.

8. Set up to cut the mortises. You can drill and chop them by hand, but routing them is much easier. I use a U-shaped, shopmade router jig to hold the workpiece, as shown in "Router Mortising Jig" on p. 147. You'll need a big router that has enough power and reach to cut these big mortises.

9. Rout each mortise, taking multiple passes and moving the router left to right. With my 3¼-hp router, I can easily cut ½ in. deep in one pass (see **photo G** on p. 146). With smaller routers, take passes of ¼ in. or less at a

you're within a hair of the scored line on the edge, the tissue-thin ribbon of wood clinging to the upper edge of the scored gauge line lets you know you only have a couple more passes to take until the line disappears.

5. Sand the bevel with 220-grit sandpaper.

Photo D: If you can't find 3-in.-thick stock to make the legs, laminate two pieces of thinner material together.

Photo E: Clamp the two leg halves together using a lot of clamps near the edges of the pieces.

Photo F: After ripping and jointing the leg blanks to thickness, crosscut them to length.

Photo G: I cut the hefty leg mortises using a 3¼-hp router with the workpiece wedged in a shopmade router mortising jig. The router edge guide runs along the outside wall of the jig.

time. After reaching the ¼-in. haunch depth, rout out the mortise for the main body of the tenon to a depth of 2¼ in.

Making the aprons

1. Dimension the apron stock to size.
2. Lay out the tenons. Mark the shoulders using an accurate square, then knife the lines. Mark the cheeks with a mortise gauge.
3. Because these large aprons can be difficult to handle on the table saw, I prefer to cut the tenons by hand, using a bowsaw. Its wide blade tracks well and cuts fast.

4. Chisel a shallow V-cut along the shoulder lines to help guide the saw, then saw the shoulders.
5. Saw the cheeks a bit fat, so you can plane them for a snug fit in their mortises afterward.
6. Clamp the aprons in a vise, angled away from you.
7. Starting at the corner of the tenon, saw diagonally until the cut extends from the shoulder to the center of the tenon (see **photo H** on p. 148).
8. Reverse the workpiece in the vise and cut from the other side in the same manner.

Router Mortising Jig

THIS SIMPLE JIG HOLDS workpieces for mortising with a router. The workpiece is wedged or clamped into the jig with its face flush with the top edge of the jig. The router rides atop the jig, with its edge guide riding against the outside wall of the jig. The jig shown here is sized for a large, 3¼-hp router. When using a smaller router, insert an auxiliary block inside the jig to decrease the wall spacing, as shown.

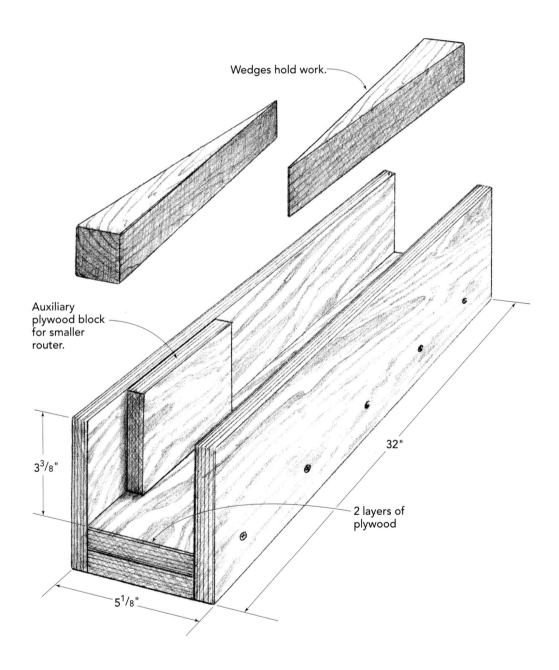

Wedges hold work.

Auxiliary plywood block for smaller router.

$3^3/8$"

32"

2 layers of plywood

$5^1/8$"

Photo H: I use a bowsaw to cut the apron tenons. I start by cutting the waste diagonally from opposing corners, then finish up by sawing straight downward toward the tenon shoulder.

Photo I: After rounding the bottom edge of the apron tenon and cutting the haunch, trim the cheeks with a rabbet plane for a snug fit in the leg mortises.

Finish the cut by sawing straight downward toward the shoulder.

9. Round the bottom edge of each tenon to match the ¼-in. radius of the mortise. I round most of the edge with a rasp, but I switch to a chisel for the section nearest the shoulder to avoid marring the apron.

10. Cut the ½-in. haunch with a handsaw.

11. Using a rabbet plane, trim each tenon to fit snugly into its mortise (see **photo I**).

12. Miter the end of each tenon to provide ⅛ in. of clearance inside the leg where the two tenons meet.

13. Rout the slots for the button blocks, This is easily done with a ⅜-in.-diameter straight bit and a router edge guide.

14. Use a smoothing plane set for a very fine cut to smooth the outside faces of the aprons and the inside faces of the legs. Follow up by sanding with 220-grit paper.

Assembling the base

1. Dry-fit the entire base together and inspect the joints for tight fit (see **photo J**).
2. Trim the joints if necessary to correct any misfits. Also use this opportunity to prepare your clamps for the glue-up.
3. Glue up the end assemblies by gluing the legs to the short aprons. Keep the clamp screw pressure in line with the aprons to prevent the legs from cocking inward.

4. After clamping, check to make sure that the legs are square to the apron (see **photo K**).
5. After the end assemblies have dried, glue them to the long aprons. Check the base for square by comparing the diagonals across the top (see **photo L** on p. 151).
6. Plane and scrape the outside faces of the legs, then sand them with 220-grit sandpaper.

Photo J: In preparation for glue-up, check the fit of the mortise-and-tenon joints, trimming them as necessary to ensure a good fit.

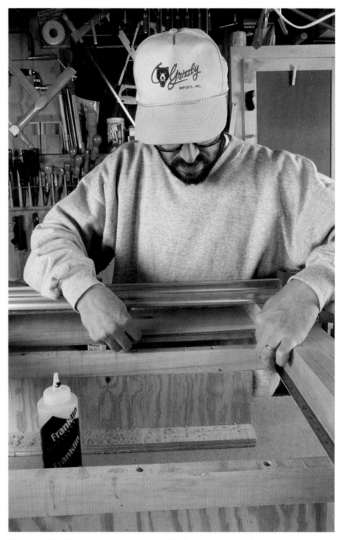

Photo K: Working on a pair of clamping stands, I clamp the short aprons to the legs, then check that the assembly is square.

Making and Attaching the Button Blocks

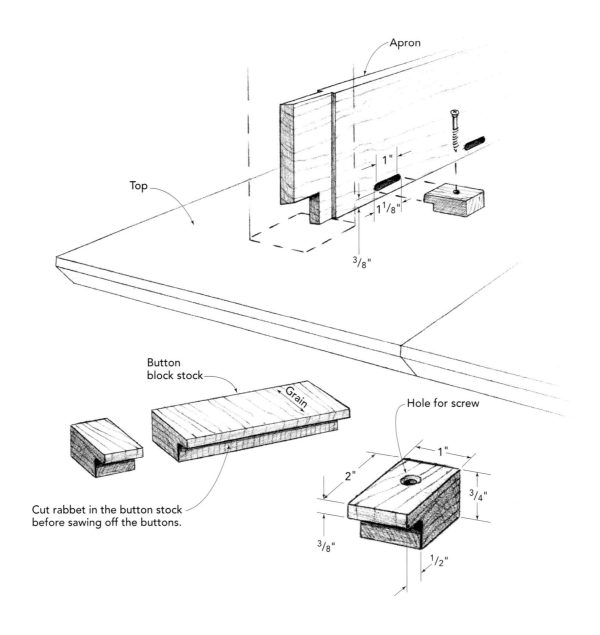

Apron

Top

1"

1 1/8"

3/8"

Button block stock

Grain

Hole for screw

Cut rabbet in the button stock
before sawing off the buttons.

1"

2"

3/4"

3/8"

1/2"

Photo L: After gluing the end assemblies to the long aprons, check the table for square by comparing the diagonals across the top.

7. Make the button blocks that fasten the tabletop to the aprons. Saw them from a piece of short-grain stock that you've rabbeted, as shown in "Making and Attaching the Button Blocks." Then drill the holes.

FINISHING UP

Klausz sprays on four coats of catalyzed varnish for a very tough finish. I used linseed oil, which is easy to repair and offers resistance to water, alcohol, and hot serving platters (see "Boiled Linseed Oil Finish" on p. 137).

1. Scrutinize all of the show surfaces of the table in preparation for finishing. Do any necessary touch-up sanding and make sure all sharp corners are slightly rounded over.
2. Apply finish to the top and base before fastening them together.
3. When you're done with the finishing, attach the top. Lay it upside down on the bench, centering the base on top of it to create an equal overhang on all sides.
4. Place the button blocks into their slots and screw them to the tabletop. Allow a ⅛-in. gap between the shoulders of the button blocks and the long aprons to allow for cross-grain movement of the top over time.

Danish Farmer's Trestle Table

Mario Rodriguez, a professional woodworker, teacher, and author, designed and built this pine trestle table. He uses it as a desk, but it could also serve as a dining or library table. The table is a hybrid interpretation of a Danish farmer's table and a similar table that Rodriguez saw at the Winterthur Gallery in Wilmington, Delaware.

The table can be built longer or shorter to suit individual needs, without disturbing its proportions. It's heavy, solid, and rugged. It can withstand a great deal of abuse—making it a good choice for people with large families. It's also likely to get better looking with age, because dents and scratches tend to complement its rustic character.

The table is fairly ornate for such a rustic piece. Curved profiles on the trestles, ogees on the battens, and the ornate molding of the beam all add wonderful character. The shaped wedges and turned pins offer further flourish. As a counterpoint to all this decoration, Rodriguez chose to use common pine, distressing the wood by sandblasting it to simulate aging.

Danish Farmer's Trestle Table

THE TOP OF THIS TABLE rests on two X-shaped trestles, connected by a beam. Battens keep the tabletop flat and provide an attachment for the trestles. Each trestle is each made from two legs that connect with half-lap notches. A beam spans the trestles and provides resistance to racking. Removable batten pins and tusk tenon wedges allow the table to be taken apart for moving.

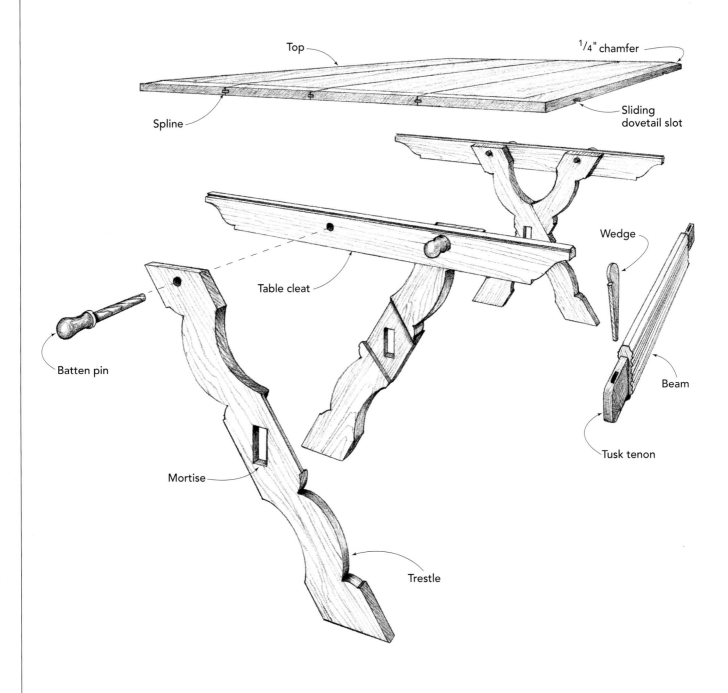

Top

¹/₄" chamfer

Spline

Sliding dovetail slot

Wedge

Table cleat

Beam

Batten pin

Tusk tenon

Mortise

Trestle

EDGE DETAIL

1/4" chamfer

SPLINE JOINT DETAIL

1 1/4"

1/2"

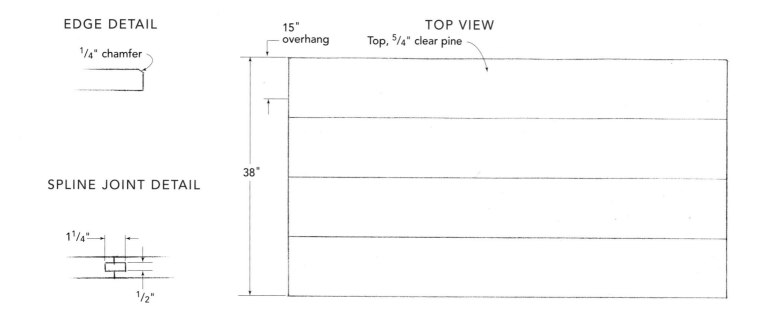

15" overhang

TOP VIEW

Top, 5/4" clear pine

38"

END VIEW

Holes for pins used to join the base to the table cleats.

4 1/8"

Mortise for beam.

Base is half-lapped at the intersection.

3"

1/4"

3"

SIDE VIEW

72"

42"

36"

1 1/4"

15"

1 1/4"

28"

7"

1 3/4"

50"

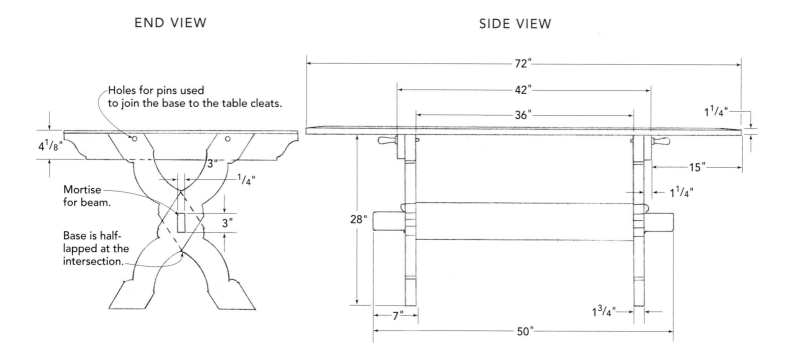

Building the Table Step-by-Step

CUT LIST FOR DANISH FARMER'S TRESTLE TABLE		
Top		
1	Plank	1¼ in. x 38 in. x 72 in.
2	Battens	1¼ in. x 4⅛ in. x 38 in.
Base		
4	Leg stock	1¾ in. x 4½ in. x 40½ in.
1	Beam	1¾ in. x 6 in. x 50 in.
Fittings		
2	Wedges	¾ in. x 1½ in. x 7 in.

THE MAIN COMPONENTS of this table are the top, the battens, the trestles, and the beam. Holding the components together are four turned pins and two tapered wedges. It's important to make the top first and then the battens. After that, you'll make the legs and beam.

Making the Top

Making the plank

1. Dimension enough stock to glue up the 1¼-in.-thick by 38-in.-wide by 72-in.-long top. Leave the stock a bit wide and long for now. You'll rip and crosscut it to final size after glue-up. Rodriguez made his top from two wide boards, but it's fine to glue up a number of narrower boards instead.
2. Joint the edges of the boards. Long boards like this are best jointed on a power jointer rather than by hand.
3. Rout or saw a ½-in. by ⅝-in. groove in all of the long edges to be joined. I find it easier to bring a router to the workpiece in this case, rather than maneuver huge boards across the table saw. If you rout using a straight bit and a router fence, clamp another board to the workpiece to provide additional router bearing surface. Alternatively, you could rout the groove with a slot-cutter bit taking several passes.
4. Make enough ½-in.-thick spline stock to join the boards, sawing it a bit fat.
5. Plane the stock to final thickness, checking its fit in the groove as you progress. It should be snug, but require only a bit of finger pressure to insert.
6. Rip the spline stock into 1¼-in.-wide strips.
7. Glue up the top, applying plenty of glue to the splines and slots. Clamp the boards together tightly. Make sure the assembly lies flat while under clamp pressure.
8. When the glue has dried thoroughly, scrape off the excess. Then plane or belt sand the top and bottom of the plank reasonably flat.
9. Rip and crosscut the top to width and length. If you can, get help ripping this heavy top on the table saw. Because it would be very difficult to crosscut on the table saw, cut the top to length with a handsaw or portable circular saw. You can guide a circular saw against a straightedge clamped to the tabletop.
10. Finish-sand the top, including its edges and then rout the ¼-in. chamfer along the top edge.

Cutting the sliding dovetail slot

A hand-cut sliding dovetail joint isn't difficult to make, but you may want to practice first on scrap if you haven't made one before.

1. Mark out the sliding dovetail slot with the top lying upside down on the bench. Using a long straightedge, draw two parallel lines 1¼ in. apart and 15 in. in from the end of the tabletop to locate each batten, as shown in "Cutting a Sliding Dovetail."

Cutting a Sliding Dovetail

FIRST CUT THE SIDES of the sliding dovetail with a dovetail saw, then chisel out the waste, and finally clean up the bottom with a router plane.

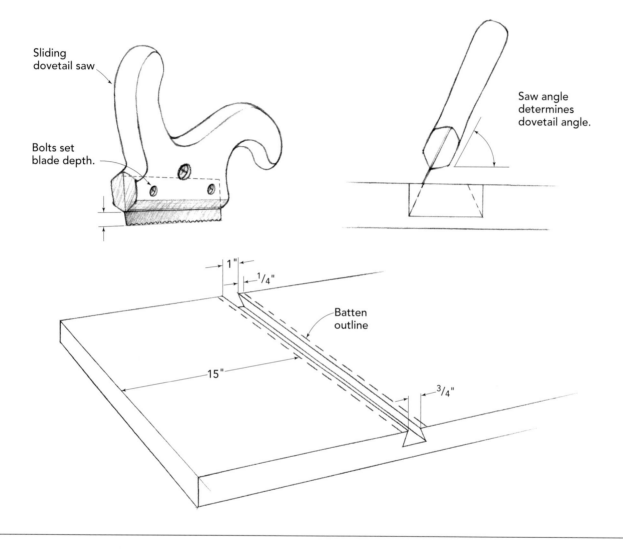

Sliding dovetail saw

Bolts set blade depth.

Saw angle determines dovetail angle.

1"

1/4"

Batten outline

15"

3/4"

2. Lay out the tapered slot, centering it between the two parallel lines that you drew. The slot tapers from 1 in. at its wide end to ¾ in. at the narrow end.

3. Score the taper marks with a knife, then chisel a shallow V-cut along each line to help guide your saw.

4. Set the blade on a sliding dovetail saw to project ⅜ in. Place the blade in your chiseled

V-cuts and saw into the line. Hold the saw so that its angled shoulder is parallel to the tabletop. Cut until the saw's shoulder contacts the workpiece.

5. After cutting the walls of the slot, chisel out the majority of the waste. Then level the bottom of the slot with a router plane (see **photo A** on p. 158). Getting a consistent depth is important to the fit of the joint.

Photo A: After sawing the walls of the tapered dovetail slot, chisel out most of the waste, and then level the bottom of the slot with a router plane.

Making and fitting the battens

1. Dimension the stock for the battens.

2. Make a plywood or hardboard template for the batten detail shown in "Batten Pattern."

3. Using the template, trace the profile onto the end of the batten stock (see **photo B**).

4. Cut the profile with a jigsaw or bandsaw.

5. Cut the sliding dovetail on the top edge of the batten using a skewed fillister (or dovetail) plane.

6. Start with short strokes, trimming the dovetail at what will be its narrower end; lengthen the strokes gradually to create the taper on one side of the batten (see **photo C**). If you don't have a dovetail plane, you can cut the majority of the tail with a rabbet plane, tilting it to make the angled cut.

7. Pare the shoulders with a chisel.

8. When one side of the dovetail is done, plane the other side. Work carefully and check the fit of the dovetail in its slot frequently. You want the dovetail to end up fitting tightly along the full length of the slot.

Photo B: Lay out the ogee on the end of each batten using a template made from "Batten Pattern."

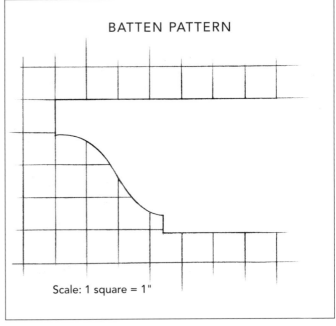

BATTEN PATTERN

Scale: 1 square = 1"

Photo C: Using a dovetail plane, cut the tapered dovetail on each batten. Begin at the narrow end of the taper, taking short strokes and working toward the wider end.

Photo D: When the dovetail is fairly snug along its length and is sitting a couple of inches from the end of the slot, it's ready to be glued and tapped home.

9. Stop planing when the batten fits fairly snugly with just a couple of inches to go (see **photo D**).

10. Spread glue in the end of the slot, then hammer the batten in until it's flush with the edge of the tabletop.

MAKING THE BASE

The base consists of two X-shaped trestles and a beam. First you'll cut out the legs and join them to make the trestles. Then you'll cut the beam mortises in the trestles and make the beam. The last thing to do is to make the tusk tenon joints to hold the trestles to the beam.

Making the trestles

1. Make a full-size plywood or hardboard template for the legs by enlarging the "Leg Pattern" (see p. 150).

2. Dimension stock for the legs.

3. Use the template to trace the shape of the legs onto the stock (see **photo E** on p. 160).

4. Cut the legs to shape on a bandsaw, following the lines carefully to minimize cleanup later. An auxiliary table clamped to the bandsaw table will help support the long pieces as you cut them.

5. Smooth the profiles of the legs using a combination of spokeshaves, rasps, and wood files (see **photo F** on p. 161). There's no need to be too fussy here—tool marks add some character to this piece. Do take care to straighten up the cuts at top and bottom of the legs, because they'll determine whether the table sits flat. There is such a thing as too much character.

6. Lay the outer leg on top of the inner leg to mark out the half-lap notches, keeping the legs' inner faces together. Make sure that the bottom of the feet are in line with each other.

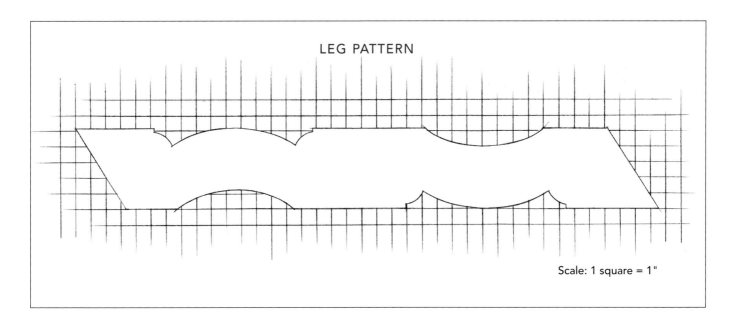

LEG PATTERN

Scale: 1 square = 1"

Photo E: Trace the profile of the leg onto its blank using a template.

7. Center the leg overlap evenly, then mark the notch on the inner leg by tracing the edges of the outer leg.

8. Cut the notches out using a bowsaw, chisels, and a router plane (see **photo G**). If you'd rather use other tools, such as a router, they'll work just fine.

9. Clean up the bottom with a rabbet plane (see **photo H**).

10. Place the unnotched leg of each trestle into the notch of the other leg. Slide it up or down in the notch until both legs are level at the bottom.

11. Lay out the notches for the second pieces and cut them out as before.

12. Glue the trestle halves together (see **photo I** on p. 162).

13. Lay out a beam mortise in the center of each trestle. To ensure that the mortise isn't tilted, stand each trestle up on your bench, then mark out the vertical walls using a large square registered against your benchtop.

14. Cut out the mortises by drilling or routing out the bulk of the material, then cleaning up the walls with a chisel.

Making the beam

1. Dimension the beam to size.

2. Clamp the trestles to the outside faces of the battens, then hold the beam up to the trestles.

3. Mark the tenon shoulder locations with a knife.

4. Completely mark out each tusk tenon, as shown in "Tusk Tenon Joint Detail" (see p. 162).

5. Saw the tenons. I used a bowsaw to cut the shoulders and cheeks and a rasp to round the ends, but whatever tools you're used to using

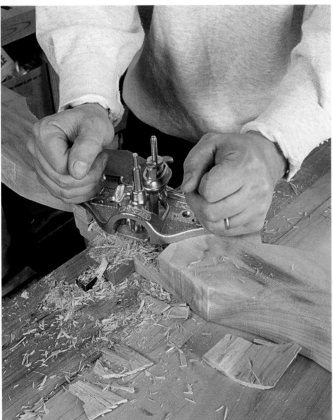

Photo F: Clean up the bandsaw marks on the leg pieces using files, rasps, and spokeshaves.

Photo G: After sawing the shoulders of the leg notches and removing most of the waste with a chisel, flatten the bottom of the notch using a router plane.

Photo H: Do the final cleaning of the notch bottom with a rabbet plane.

Tusk Tenon Joint Detail

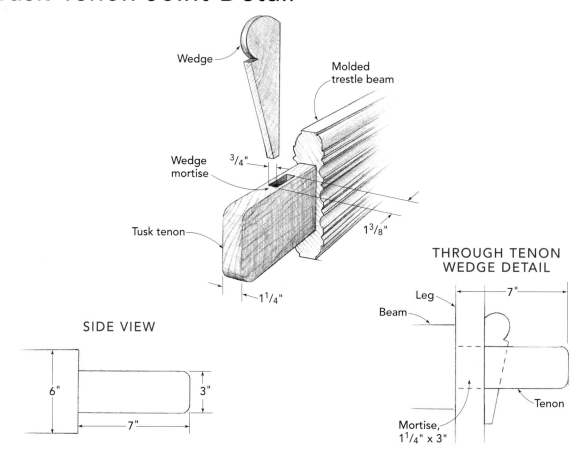

Wedge

Molded trestle beam

Wedge mortise

3/4"

Tusk tenon

1 3/8"

1 1/4"

SIDE VIEW

6"

3"

7"

THROUGH TENON WEDGE DETAIL

Leg

Beam

7"

Tenon

Mortise, 1 1/4" x 3"

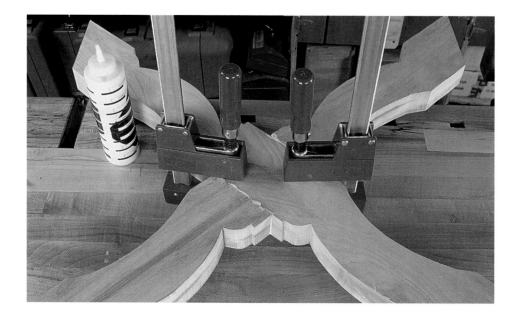

Photo I: Glue and clamp the two leg sections together to create the X-shaped trestles.

Routing the Beam Profile

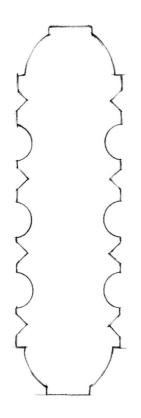

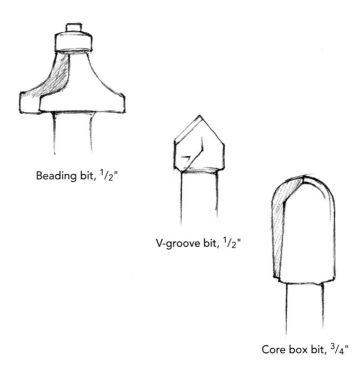

Beading bit, $1/2$"

V-groove bit, $1/2$"

Core box bit, $3/4$"

for this work will do just fine. It's not necessary to fine-tune the fit of the shoulders to the mortise because the joint gains its strength from the mechanical force of the shoulder wedged against the trestle.

Making the tusk tenon joint

1. Fit the beam into its mortises, then clamp the trestles tight to the tenon shoulders.

2. Mark the top and bottom edges of the tenon by tracing along the outside faces of the trestle with a sharp pencil.

3. Remove the beam and mark another line $1/16$ in. in from each of your pencil lines toward the tenon shoulder.

4. Connect the lines, extending them across the tenon cheeks. These are your layout lines

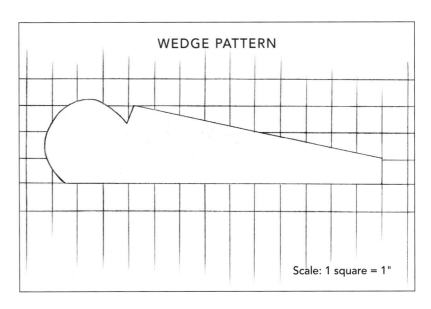

WEDGE PATTERN

Scale: 1 square = 1"

for the innermost wall of the wedge mortise. The mortise is inset from the leg to ensure that the joint will pull up tight.

5. Make the wedges on a bandsaw or a scroll-saw or with a jigsaw, as shown in "Wedge Pattern" on p. 163.

6. Lay the wedge on the mortise cheek with the top of the wedge sitting about 2¼ in. from the top of the tenon, and the back of the wedge against the layout line.

7. Trace the wedge slope onto the cheek, then extend slope line squarely across the top and bottom of the tenon.

8. Drilling straight down on the drill press, drill out as much waste as possible from the wedge tenon. Then pare the slope with a sharp chisel, being careful not to split the tenon.

9. Replace the beam into the trestle mortises and check the fit of the wedges. Pare each sloped mortise wall as necessary to provide full contact of the wedge against the slope, with both wedges projecting about the same amount from their mortises.

10. Shape the beam with a handheld router, router guide, and the bits shown in "Routing the Beam Profile" on p. 163. Rodriguez used molding planes for this. Your molding doesn't have to match the drawing's exactly; it's just important that the beam is molded to your liking.

ASSEMBLING THE TABLE

1. Turn the batten pins to the dimensions shown in "Batten Pin." I roughed out a small ¾-in.-diameter cylinder and turned the handle curves, then I took a planing cut with a skew chisel to turn the slight taper (see **photo J**).

BATTEN PIN

⅝"

9/16"

4 "

6½"

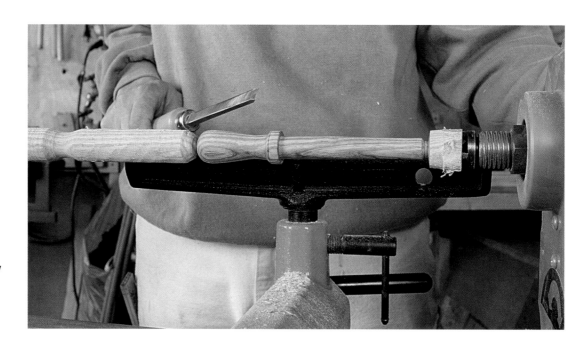

Photo J: Use a skew chisel to turn the slight taper on the batten pins.

2. Assemble the trestles and the beam, tapping the wedges firmly into their mortises (see **photo K**).

3. Center the tabletop in place on top of the trestles and clamp the trestles to the battens.

4. Drill a hole through the top of each leg and its batten (see **photo L**). Clamp a backer block on the backside of the batten to prevent tearout.

5. Tap the pins into their holes to complete the assembly of the table.

FINISHING UP

Apply the finish of your choice. Rodriguez stained his table with a homemade finish. I suggest using a dark-tinted oil, like Watco dark walnut Danish oil (available at many hardware and paint stores), applying three or four coats.

Photo K: Assemble the trestles and the beam by tapping the tusk tenon wedges into place.

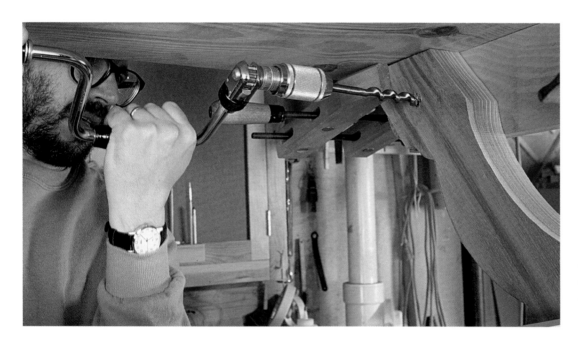

Photo L: Clamp the trestles to the battens and then drill the holes for the batten pins.

SOURCES

CONSTANTINE'S
2050 Eastchester Rd.
Bronx, NY 10461
(800) 223-8087
*Veneer, veneering supplies, and
woodworking supplies*

GARRETT WADE
161 Ave. of the Americas
New York, NY 10013
(800) 221-2942
*Southerland Welles polymerized tung oil;
specialty woodworking tools and supplies*

HIGHLAND HARDWARE
1045 N. Highland Ave. NE
Atlanta, GA 30306
(800) 241-6748
*Hydrocote water-based finishes, tools,
and woodworking supplies*

LARRY & FAYE BRUSSO CO.
4865 Highland Rd., Suite J
Waterford MI 48328
(248) 674-8458
*Knife hinges, bullet catches, and other
specialty brass hardware*

LEE VALLEY TOOLS, LTD.
P.O. Box 1780
Ogdensburg, NY 13669-9973
(800) 871-8158
Hardware, tools, and woodworking supplies

McFEELY'S
1620 Wythe Rd.
Lynchburg, VA 24506-1169
(800) 443-7937
*Square drive screws, fasteners, drill bits,
tools, and woodworking supplies*

ROCKLER
4365 Willow Dr.
Medina MN, 55340
(800) 279-4441
Hardware, tools, and woodworking supplies

WHITECHAPEL, LTD.
P.O. Box 136
Wilson, WY 83014
(800) 468-5534
*Reproduction period hardware, cut nails, and
Tried and True varnish oil*

WOODCRAFT
120 Wood Country Industrial Park
P.O. Box 1686
Parkersburg, WV 26102-1686
(800) 225-1153
*Specialty woods, polyurethane glue,
Watco Danish oil, hardware, tools, and
woodworking supplies*

WOODWORKER'S SUPPLY
1108 N. Glen Rd.
Casper, WY 82601
(800) 645-9292
Hardware, tools, and woodworking supplies

METRIC CONVERSION CHART

INCHES	CENTIMETERS	MILLIMETERS	INCHES	CENTIMETERS	MILLIMETERS
⅛	0.3	3	13	33.0	330
¼	0.6	6	14	35.6	356
⅜	1.0	10	15	38.1	381
½	1.3	13	16	40.6	406
⅝	1.6	16	17	43.2	432
¾	1.9	19	18	45.7	457
⅞	2.2	22	19	48.3	483
1	2.5	25	20	50.8	508
1¼	3.2	32	21	53.3	533
1½	3.8	38	22	55.9	559
1¾	4.4	44	23	58.4	584
2	5.1	51	24	61.0	610
2½	6.4	64	25	63.5	635
3	7.6	76	26	66.0	660
3½	8.9	89	27	68.6	686
4	10.2	102	28	71.1	711
4½	11.4	114	29	73.7	737
5	12.7	127	30	76.2	762
6	15.2	152	31	78.7	787
7	17.8	178	32	81.3	813
8	20.3	203	33	83.8	838
9	22.9	229	34	86.4	864
10	25.4	254	35	88.9	889
11	27.9	279	36	91.4	914
12½	30.5	305			

INDEX

INDEX